The Cc
Parei

Highlights & Commentary on Dr. Leonard Sax's Diagnosis & Time Proven Solutions for Family Life

Nate Richardson

Nate Richardson is a member of The Church of Jesus Christ of Latter-day Saints. He is the editor of RichardsonStudies.com. His writing focuses on faith-based research & philosophy.

Some of Nate's parenting background includes many years of fostering children from diverse backgrounds, caring for many children at home, many years teaching at a youth from around the country at a treatment center, and formal university training on the subject.

Contents

About this Book

Dr. Leonard Sax is a family physician MD and a PhD in psychology. He has conducted more than 90,000 office visits as a practicing physician between 1989 and today. He has given hundreds of lectures on parenting and related topics around the world. His other books are "Girls on the Edge," "Boys Adrift," and "Why Gender Matters." His work is well researched and easy to read. Contact him at leonardsax@gmail.com and https://www.leonardsax.com/.

These are my notes and impressions of the book and do not represent all ideas of the book. When I add my commentary I preface it with *"Note- ..."* I don't put many sources he cites into these notes, please refer to the full text for related studies. He also shares many more fun and helpful stories than I report here, as my intent is to quickly highlight a few key principles.

Overview

Do parents have authority? If so, how can they use it in ways that kids will respond to? The answer is a resounding yes, and there are many simple natural ways for parents to set limits with their children.

Dr. Sax has toured around the world and discovered that America is probably the worst when it comes to permissive parenting. America uses medication as a first option to treat kids, abdicating parental responsibility to a psychiatrist instead.

Dr. Sax has seen hundreds of cases of parents who treat kids like the kid is the boss, and the parent their slave. This isn't good for the child or the parent. Parents have a special place in the life of children as both friends and leaders, but we are lacking in the leadership aspect. Kids are walking on their parents regarding food, school, friends, and about everything else.

In the face of a society that says anything goes, a society afraid to say 'no' and afraid to use their instincts, Dr. Sax brings a refreshing voice of reason to empower parents to do what they were always meant to do: to lead their kids toward responsibility.

Dr. Sax points out that for authoritative parenting to work the parent has to have authority. The parents used to be the ones in charge, but now the kids raise each other, and there's a culture of disrespect and rudeness the children have toward everyone, toward their parents and even their peers. They rely on their peers to raise them, not their parents. They think that the parents don't deserve to know what's going on in their lives. They think they should be the one who gets to choose what school to go to etc. but parents used to be the ones who decided all this. Parents aren't really parents anymore.

Note- As we get started I'll mention that I have a concern that he might suggest that the age before adulthood is quite old such as mid-20s. Of course, many today do. He correctly defines adolescence as the time between when someone can have children and when they are adults, but I think it is dangerous to have a longer and longer expectation of kids to be biological adults (puberty) without being cultural adults. I foresee a future where culture will have increasing respect for mature youths as adults in society. Today our youth simply aren't mature whatsoever. This is the situation we are dealing with, but as we apply correct parenting over a few generations, it will likely become common to see much more mature and responsible 'young' people.

From Dr. Sax you'll learn that you can explain your expectations, but you don't need to negotiate. Parents must command. You'll learn that American kids are more disrespectful to their teachers than students elsewhere around the world. In Australia when a student leaves  the classroom they say, "thank you sir" or "thank you ma'am" or "great lesson."

Some think it is going to allow for higher creativity in America to allow students to be so disrespectful, but not so.

You'll learn that America is unique in using all the technical gadgets in the classroom. There's no proof that these actually help. We don't need to turn the classroom into an arcade room! Other countries without this stuff are doing way better in education even though America spends more on education. Education is less about technology and more about respect for teachers, and good teachers.

You'll learn powerful tips like don't let your kid go to another kid's house where violent video games are played. It's ok to be the only kid without a cell phone throughout high school. The parent's job of limit setting etc. is more important than the kid liking the parent.

Part 1: Problems

Introduction: Parents Adrift

American kids are now less resilient, more fragile, more overweight, and more likely to be diagnosed with mental problems. Surprisingly, all of this can be traced to the loss of the art of parenting.

Over the past three decades there has been a **massive transfer of authority** from parents to kids. "Let kids decide" has become a mantra of good parenting. What the kid believes and wants is now seen as important or more than what the parent sees as best.
These well-intentioned changes are profoundly harmful to kids.

If a kid is hungry enough, he will eat essential healthy foods. Parents today are so timid that they allow kids to refuse healthy foods routinely, so the kids get poor health from vitamin deficiencies etc.

Parents are letting kids (as young as 8) decide which school to go to against their better judgment. Parents today mistakenly think that being a good parent means letting kids choose everything. They think that parents can't make all the decisions for them, or they won't learn how to decide on their own.

Note – Obviously there's some truth to the importance of allowing kids to make choices, but parents must intervene in big choices. A parent is particularly responsible for a child under its roof. Parents know best and are accountable before God for righteously rearing their children. Ultimately if a kid wants to go off the deep end when they move out, that's not the parent's problem. But as you'll see as we continue on in this book, kids raised with responsibility often don't leave the roost to sew wild oats, it's typically the kids raised without limits that sew the wildest oats as both adolescents and young adults.

Today's parents are unwilling to force a child to go to a certain school because they don't want to deal with the complaining that might ensue. 40 years ago, parents would not let the kid choose and would **overrule the kid's preference for the kids' sake**. Today it is common to let a kid have the final say.

One dad saw drunk kids at his house, he bought a breathalyzer and called a kids parents to bring him home. Surprisingly the parents were upset that the parent did this, thinking that it was okay for underage drinking at people's houses, making the argument that 'they're going to do it anyway.' One mother who advocated letting kids drink at a young age 'because they're going to do it anyway' was seen picking her child up from school, and when she asked the kid how he was doing, the kid said, "turn around, shut up and drive." And she did. As you now see, the permissive 'they're going to do it anyway' approach gives children a toxic sense of entitlement. Parents must step up and make demands on their children's conduct!

Ch. 1 The Culture of Disrespect

Humans are different from animals because of culture. Customs are learned and differ between communities.

Kindergarteners are being pushed to be less playful and more academically rigorous, and this is not good. As a result of this backwards approach to child development, kids aren't learning proper socialization. Basics like don't hit, share, and clean up aren't being learned.

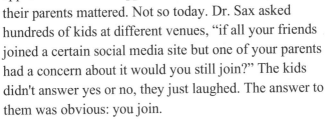

It used to be that kids wouldn't join a club if their parents didn't approve because the approval of their parents mattered. Not so today. Dr. Sax asked hundreds of kids at different venues, "if all your friends joined a certain social media site but one of your parents had a concern about it would you still join?" The kids didn't answer yes or no, they just laughed. The answer to them was obvious: you join.

Note- social media on phones is one of the most toxic influencers of our time, and Dr. Sax points this out excellently in this book. Elder Packer taught this out in a pointed way: "Largely because of television, instead of looking over into that spacious building, we are, in effect, living inside of it. That is your fate in this generation. You are living in that great and spacious building." (President Boyd K. Packer Jan. 16 2007

Lehi's Dream and You - Boyd K. Packer - BYU Speeches)

Parents are reluctant to insist that time with family is more important than time with same-age-peers. Parents are suffering from role confusion; they are unsure what authority they have and how to exercise it. Kids attitudes toward parents these days are ingratitude and contempt.

It used to be that kids would learn right and wrong at schools, but not so anymore.

Note- children's books these days don't even try to teach morals. Their only aim is to make the book as entertaining as possible to sell the most books possible and to just 'get the kids to read.' what is this, the Soviet Union? Maybe we should assign them all Mao's Little Red Book if we don't care about the content. We might as well. They don't dare include any moral teachings in the books just in case that would offend some kids or bore some kids.

Note - I went to a school assembly a few years ago where a young author told a story about how when he first released his popular nonsense kids books, an old man marched up to him and scolded him for making these books which teach no morals. When this account was told, the audience at the assembly all laughed at the old man. But I agree with the old man. Authors and influencers (especially parents) have a moral obligation to teach good morals throughout all of their teachings. Parents have a duty to permeate the family culture with truth and light. I believe the author remembered and retold this story because deep down, he knows the old man is right. Bravo to the old man who spoke up!

Note - It is ironic to me how the bible and biblical teachings are the one thing we should be teaching the most, and yet they have become the one thing no one dares to teach! God forbid you write something of a moral or religious nature into your children's book! Perhaps the fear of making less sales is driving this lack of faith in literature. Well has it been written that the love of money is the root of all evil! Perhaps the timid author fears man, but woe to such! The righteous author shouldn't give one hoot about whether 1 or 1 million people read his book; his only objective should be to write a book that God would be proud of.

When kids misbehave it's less controversial to suggest that the kid has oppositional defiance disorder or hyperactivity disorder than to suggest that the parents need to train the kid. School administrators and physicians point to diagnosis and medication rather than telling parents to train their kid to have social skills.

Parents today shoulder a greater burden than prior generations now that they are the only ones teaching social skills. And they have less tools to do it.

Parental authority isn't all about enforcing with discipline. Parental authority is about a scale of value, that parents matter more than same-age-peers.

For the majority of human history, kids have learned culture from adults. Now they are learning it from other kids. Kids today have their own culture, the culture of disrespect. They learn it from their peers and teach it to their peers.

Note- I believe Jesus said something about this when he said if the blind lead the blind, they will both fall into the ditch.

Several decades ago, the popular song was "I want to hold Your hand." Today the popular song is "I want to **** you." A radio edit version played, but the extremely popular version was the uncensored version. It reached number one in the United States.

Note- still think the US is a Christian nation? Elder Cook put it softly when he said, "The goal of honoring the Lord and submitting ourselves to His will is not as valued in today's society as it has been in the past. Some Christian leaders of other faiths believe we are living in

*a **post-Christian world**." (Elder Quinton L. Cook, 2017 Oct. Gen. Conf. "The Eternal Everyday" The Eternal Everyday (churchofjesuschrist.org))*

Kids wear t-shirts saying "do I look like I care," "out of your league," "find me another drink you're still ugly," "I don't need you I have Wi-Fi," and "you looked better on Facebook."

The Disney channel actively promotes disrespect and undermines the authority of parents. Its shows depict parents being frequently absent and ignorant when compared to the kids. Talking animals are shown to be more insightful than fathers. In the 1960s through the 1980s parents were shown as competent leaders. There are no kids  shows these days that depict parents as reliable and trustworthy!

Two generations ago, American teachers taught right and wrong in plain terms. Do to others what you would have done to you.

Note – in my work as a schoolteacher I am shocked to encounter many kids who say "I only respect people who respect me;" they've missed the whole point of respect… they see no problem with treating others poorly that they don't like. They are quick to find fault with others and justify their extreme rudeness and disrespect. I used to wonder how societies would accept Hitlers and the like, now it's not so hard to figure out. My students from all around the country typically demonstrate a disturbing rejection of both human rights and the rule of law. It's no wonder when they've been programmed with Marxist television programs their whole lives.

Note - The author points out how kids are starting to tell teachers to "shut up." That is completely unacceptable but let me just say it's much worse than that. There's a tragic trend in limiting teachers in giving any sort of corrective consequences for bad behaviors, and the schools are becoming zoos where the teachers are the doormats. Kids spend 8 hours a day at such places where the adults have no real authority; is it any wonder they go home and treat their parents with contempt?

Parents and teachers today don't command - instead they ask, and question. Naturally kids answer with the answer they know parents want to hear and dismiss the parent as something to be toyed with. We can only communicate our culture to the next generation if we assert our authority.

Note – yes, it is a righteous thing to use authority and pass on wholesome culture. What's going to happen to them if we don't? They'll be eaten by the wolves. The culture war will be lost.

Prolonged childhood in humans is how culture is passed on. When parents mean more than peers, the parents can teach right and wrong in a meaningful way. Parents can help each child to develop a stable sense of self based on the child's nature and mission rather than social media likes. Parents are the ones who can instill a love for (real) music, (real) art, and (real) education.

Note- much of what is listened to today could not be classified as real (certainly not celestial) music. The same goes for art. Parents can help kids mow past all the weeds (pushed by kids and some adults) so they can get to the real fruit. Beware that every movie, every song, every TV program is education. So what are your kids learning? High culture or pop culture? Pay close attention to the attitudes in these programs, etc. If we aren't careful, a lifetime of brainwashing will be instilled to our kids right under our noses in our own homes and using the devices we gave them.

In 20th century Europe and America, every kind of authority became suspect. While it's great that people got rights and equality, we forgot that children shouldn't be treated the same as adults.

Note - Adults are the leaders of children, not their equals. Parents must preside over their children. The fact that this must be said, and it does need to be said, is itself alarming.

Note- responsibility always comes with rights. Maybe we should hatch up a "Bill of Responsibilities."

In America we think new means better. You even see it in our architecture; it's more common in America than elsewhere to tear down old buildings to put new ones up.

Note- some of that of course is related to our prosperity and ability to upgrade, but it's still a good point; we are losing respect for all things old (including people). Its also puzzling why we are voting for our government to spend more and more debt based money we don't have to replace old buildings with new, etc. We also can't seem to come up with a school textbook that's good for more than 2 years.

In America **we value youth more than maturity**, and this undermines the authority of parents. Our celebration of youth for youth's sake is more pronounced than anywhere else. Our products are advertised as being good because they are newer. Our billboards advertise plastic surgeons to make you look younger. You don't see these things in Europe and elsewhere.

Progress now means taking away from man what ennobles him and selling it cheaply for what debases him!

In other countries people know the stories of their ancestors, the history of their country, and they speak of it with pride. They wear the clothes of their parents (the kilts etc.) whenever the occasion arises. Could you imagine American youth wearing the clothes of their ancestors?

Parents mistakenly think that a child is being independent when they skip a family vacation to go stay at a friend's house. They are still dependent, they're just **transferring that dependency from their parents to their peers.** Thus the child's top priorities become pleasing their peers. Parents become an afterthought, a means to another end. (Someone the child doesn't feel a need to speak to or serve.)

It's hard to say no to a child that you love, but parents must do this.

Note- this is called tough love, which is an essential element of wholesome love. This is why parenting can be excruciating at times. To express your love, you have to say no, and the child likely won't fully understand for a long time. Parents must help underdeveloped people to  *make good decisions in the vulnerable stages where they aren't aware of the dangers, etc.*

Today in the US and Canada kids' primary attachment is to other kids. If most of the good times happen when kids are spending time with other kids, it's no wonder that kids won't want to spend time with adults. Parental authority needs to be exercised *(as in "we are doing this family activity and yes you're coming" or "no tonight is a family night you're staying home" or "no I don't feel like that's a good activity" or "we are doing this work project today" etc.)* so that the kid has positive experiences with the parents rather than all spare time for positive things being with peers.

Note – one tip for parents is to find ways to bring their kids with them to business meetings, to work projects, on errands, to church meetings, etc. Have them help with adult things, this is how they become adults. People might thing you are strange for bringing a child along, and you can be bold about this – my kid comes, or I'm not coming (for example, to a church youth event which your child is too young for). Usually people will relent and allow some children to come along with you make this priority known. Of course you'll have to assure them that the child will not be disruptive, and that'll require training beforehand of how to be good mannered. Parents need to prioritize their time with their kids, heaven knows there are enough times when they can't be with the kids, so make waves in pushing to get your kids involved as much as you can. A great example of this is James Stoddard as taught in the Christ Centered Home book, available at JosephSmithFoundation.org.) Finally, if your child is continually bombarded with peers and family culture is not getting passed on, you might want to consider moving to a more rural area, or homeschooling.

Note- the same goes for marriage when it comes to prioritizing recreation with family above peers - ensure you're involved in those fun times, not just your spouse going off to play with other adults without you all the time. Each spouse must respect the other enough to insist that the other be involved in recreational activities on a regular basis, and that activities beyond the scope of the family are limited.

For the first time kids are turning not to parents, teachers and other responsible adults for direction. Nature *(God)* never intended peers to be the principle guide. Kids cannot make each other mature. *(Again, the blind can't lead the blind.)*

Many kids today feel their life is none of their parents' business, and that the parent is intruding whenever the parent tries to speak with them. Kids are rude to their parents but cheerful with their peers, a sign that it's a relationship problem. This withdrawl from family indicates that the child is no longer attaching to the parents, only to the peers.

If you're just trying to get your kids to love you rather than trying to train them morally, the odds are you won't accomplish either.

Note- well said, there will always be a more fun exciting parent, or a more fun and exciting peer group a child can be spending their time. So the parent must do its duty to teach morals, to create wholesome recreation as a family, and to limit peer time. This is a leap of faith, and requires patience to wait for the results to come. Even if full desired results don't come, the parent must do it's duty. But my testimony is that these methods do in fact build family bonds, even when there are hard chapters of transitioning from pop culture to high culture, which is the duty of parents.

Note – Passing on culture from parents to children is what it means to 'think celestial,' it is to rise above pop culture and seek God's higher culture, and parents are not a negotiable element of that mission. Of course the state wants to remove kids from the influence of parents and bring them into their own version of culture, which is very different from God's culture. Some have called corrupt governments the 'church of the Devil' due to the impact they have on eliminating the family and foisting secular philosophies on the masses.

Parents are to instruct, lead and even command their children. Everything is out of balance when this is switched around and the child is the boss. **Parents who put their child's wishes first only earn their child's contempt.** But parents who are responsible in their duties to train their children do find that typically their children love and respect them for that.

Note – the Holy Ghost also aids righteous parents in their mission to build relationships in the context of proper ethics, which are often difficult to demonstrate teach and expect.

Children who get what they want when they want it, who live in the culture of pure disrespect, are not well equipped to handle the pressures of growing up into adulthood. Sometimes you have to wait before you get to eat the donuts, and sometimes you don't get to eat the donuts at all - that's life.

Ch. 2 Why Are So Many Kids Overweight

Child obesity is rampant because of defiant attitudes of children, and parents giving in, giving them whatever they want. Let's now take a closer look at these issues.

The trend of obesity in kids started in the 1970s and continued through the mid-2000s. Obese kids (obese not merely overweight) have gone from 4% to 19.6% in less than 4 decades.

The New York times bragged about Michelle Obama's kid exercise program being successful, but all that happened was very young children 2-5 weren't quite as obese, and soon their obesity reverted back to the obesity rate of the 2000s, still not where they should be. There was no data for older children.

Fitness is not the same thing as slenderness. Many skinny kids can't run a quarter mile without huffing and puffing.
Fitness for American kids was 52.4% in 1999 and 2000, but in 2012 it fell to 42%. (This study controlled for economic status, race etc.)

A pediatric preventive cardiac clinic is a new thing.

The norm in America as recently as the 1970s was that kids eat what's for supper, or they go hungry. Nowadays kids choose what's for supper.

Note – Nutrition is another excellent example of where kids simply aren't mature enough to be making these serious life long decisions! Let parents be parents! Restore their authority! Don't confuse agency with training! Parents will regret letting their children indulge in excessive behaviors with no repercussions.

Family diet standards used to include no dessert until you eat your vegetables and no snacking between meals.

The number of times American families eat at fast food restaurants has recently increased over 200%.
Note – one recent study suggested that Americans are, for the first time in history, now spending more eating at restaurants than on food from grocery stores.

Michelle Obama made a school policy on junk food, providing more healthy food. The results included lots of healthy food in the trash can, and a lot less kids getting school lunch *(Note – not that public schools should be providing meals anyway.)*. Michelle said schools should put more effort into marketing healthy food, but kids today grow up in a culture where their desires are paramount. Kids are used to eating junk food and that won't be easy to change. In affluent neighborhoods kids are bringing their own unhealthy lunches to school. **Just offering healthy choices (while still offering unhealthy ones) won't result in consistent healthy choices**! It's good that we are trying to get school food more healthy, but it doesn't work when kids are so entitled that they can still access junk food.

Note- this is one of the reasons public schools are so toxic, even the food is toxic! Of course the attitudes they learn there are even more toxic. In so many ways, public schools are portraying the philosophy to kids that they can get whatever they want. How likely is your child to choose water over wine at these institutions? You can't just offer kids luxury vs humility and expect them to consistently chose the more virtuous path. I think it borders on the unreasonable to think that these little bodies could consistently say 'no' to such toxicity all around them day in and day out. Let's face it, our kids are addicted to the junk food they've been exposed to for years at school (and to the extent of our ignorance and permisivity, exposure at home.)

*Note - Parents, protect your children! You no longer live in a wholesome society! Times have changed, wake up! The end is near! This introduces one of the mighty themes of this book: you can't offer your kids both virtue and vice. **You have to restrict the vice.** You are a guardian, not a butler! You have to show them by their experience the benefits of virtue over vice. As the prophets say, they must 'stand in holy places' so they can gain experiences with the Holy Ghost, so that when they encounter the lower realm, they'll recognize it for what it is.*

Note - We are like generals sending soldiers out to war without any training or armor when we think the state will raise our kids into proper adulthood with any sort of

27

morals intact. When I was a very small child, my much older siblings asked me what I should do when I encounter 'the bad guys.' I said, 'you get the bad guys!' Children shouldn't be expected to survive against the sophisticated amoral atheistic Marxist philosophers prevalent in our society. Yes there are monsters out there, and children were never intended to stand against them. It's the adults who must do this. Children need protection. Teach children of the evils, prepare them, instill morals into them, and yes they will eventually be out on their own. But when you compare today's parenting standards to that of the more righteous past, parents were much more actively involved in maintaining the morals of their children at home, and set more limits on their children. Add to this the corruption of our time, which increases all the more the need for parents to shelter and protect their children.

School lessons are often presented as entertainment. University professors are graded by students based on how much fun their classes are.

Parents are now carrying bags of snacks for the drive to and from the school, heaven forbid the kid experiences one minute of hunger. Parents are overly concerned about kids becoming hypoglycemic. Animals with **free access to food become fatter** than animals with scheduled access to food even when it's the **same amount** of food they eat. Kids who never experience hunger will grow up to be fatter and psychologically weaker.

Rather than only allowing dessert for eating all their broccoli, it now becomes 'ok you can have dessert after you eat 3 bites of broccoli.' Parental standards are slipping.

Parents beg their children to eat greens and the kid then feels like they've done their parent a favor if they do so, and that their parent owes them something. **So don't ask or beg, you have to tell.** Restrict rewards when they don't comply.

Note – how is this to be done? Make the first course a salad. The next course something else healthy. Finally if there is a desert, it's simply not available to those who didn't eat the healthy food.

Note: Church activities these days typically have toxic food every time. How long can we pray for these curses to be blessed? Are we so weak that we must rely on these addictive lures to get any participation from the youth? It is better to lose a few inherently disinterested youth than to poison the lot. Let the Holy Ghost convert them, not the unholy deserts. I think the main problem is 'they know not what they do' when these things are served. Hopefully the saints can mature in their understanding of the word of wisdom, and start being more wise about our culture of foods. D&C 89 lists the need for fruits vegetables and limiting meats, and these injunctions are given to even 'the weakest of saints,' so yes, we can get the youth in on this too. Of course it starts with ourselves. One heroic example in Latter-day Saint church history is that of George Albert Smith, who brought a jar of wheat to eat whenever he traveled, even refusing elaborate meals prepared for him by others.

Soon word will spread about your preferences, and this higher culture will become the new norm. The transition will, of course, hurt; that is one of the crosses of our time. Now let me have some mercy here and echo the sentiment of Henry B Eyring when he said, "I can't be a perfect servant every hour, but I can do more than I thought I could." That is our aim.

The average American child now spends 50 hours a week in front of a screen. 70 for the teenager. 1.5 hours of TV a day is typical. Just a generation ago **kids spent all their time playing outside** and only came in for meals. One mother asked her child "it's such a beautiful day, why don't you go play outside?" The child responded sincerely "but where would I plug in my Xbox?" Children now have less time for play than they used to and the play is more likely to be organized and supervised by grownups. But the biggest change is now kids would prefer a screen. Back in the day a family had one TV set so they were at least watching TV together, and there were only a few TV shows available, and they were wholesome. Not so today.

Many schools have banned dodgeball due to theoretical liability bullying & self-esteem issues. In 1969, 41% of kids walked or rode their bike to school. By 2001 it dropped to 13%.
If there's a grocery store within a mile of your home, take a daily or every other day walk to it with your kids, and carry the groceries home.

Less sleep at night means more obesity, and particularly so for children. When you're very tired your brain plays tricks on you and says 'I'm very tired I deserve/need junk food to keep going.' Ages 2-5 need 11 hours a day of sleep. 6-12 need 10 hours. 13-18 at least nine. Yet typically at 10 they're only getting 9 hours, age 15 are only getting 7.3 hours, age 17 are only getting 6.9 hours. Age 6 to 18 kids are sleep deprived. American kids are getting significant less sleep now than 20 years ago. Since 2011 affluent American Kids are reporting that their favorite thing to do by themselves is sleep.

Note – overloading schedules is a major contribution of youth (and parental) exhaustion, even including extensive play dates or unrestricted time with peers, which can't afford the general restfulness and reflection/pondering which home can provide. Constantly performing for peers or others outside the home is particularly exhausting.

American kids have screens in their bedrooms and they don't have self-control to turn those off when it's time to sleep. The bedroom should be for sleeping. When the AAP came out with guidelines to not have screens in the bedroom, the **media just mocked it as an impossible standard.**
Note- the restored Church has long taught not to have screens in bedrooms too.

Here is the root of these problems: **The culture of disrespect** leads to kids not eating vegetables, kids not doing chores, more likely to play video games, and less likely to sleep when they should.

Many studies indicate that chronically defiant and disrespectful kids are 3x as likely to become obese as respectful kids. Slender kids who are disrespectful were 5x as likely to become obese. Many parents today give in when their defiant kids insist on junk food. A '90s study in In New Zealand showed some of the defiant kids are skinnier because the parents decide what's for supper, and if the defiant kid doesn't want it, they go to bed hungry.

Ch. 3 Why Are So Many Kids on Medication?

Defiance of the kids is also leading to more diagnosis of ADHD and pediatric bipolar diagnosis. It's normal for kids to get mad and have mood swings, it's not necessarily bipolar disorder. But parents don't know how to deal with these behaviors, so they're turning to diagnosis and medication. Parents need to set and enforce consistent rules, limits and consequences.

Kindergarten classes used to teach respect, courtesy and manners; now they're just teaching grammar. Many parents today aren't equipped to teach the kids these things, so we have kids who are never learning them. Parents today don't teach common rules of  civility to their kids because for one, their parents didn't need to teach it to them, and for two, they're uncomfortable asserting parental authority.

The job of the parent is to teach self-control, to teach what is and is not acceptable, to establish boundaries and enforce consequences. Two decades ago that was common sense.

Note – it's high time for the parents to recognize the need to fulfill this role, and equip themselves to do it. Don't expect the child you ship to school every day to learn good behavior.

In '94 it was unheard of for someone under 20 to be diagnosed with bipolar. For every 1 kid diagnosed with bipolar in 1994, 43 kids were diagnosed with it in 2003.

Bipolar is typically weeks to months for each cycle, and in America they are saying for kids it happens in just a few minutes - they call it rapid cycling. Mood swings between energetic and irritable is normal for kids, it is not bipolar! They want to give your kids Risperdal, Seroquel, and other adult bipolar drugs.

Kids who have not been disciplined are going to scream in the toy store for the toy. **It's easier to resort to medication than competent authority-based parenting**. Temper tantrums are increasingly being diagnosed as psychiatric disorders like bipolar ADHD and Asperger. When parents abdicate authority, a vacuum results, and nature doesn't like vacuums. Medications fill the role that the parents should have fulfilled.

The book highlights a doctor who accepted tons of money from a drug company to push these diagnoses and drugs to the kids. Follow the yellow brick road folks.

Over-diagnoses and over-medication of kids for psychiatric disorders is mostly a problem in America. In the same period where bipolar in children was exploding in America, it was decreasing in Germany and Spain.

Europeans are skeptical about whether US kids really have bipolar. **For every one child in England given a bipolar diagnosis, 73 in the US are**.

ADHD is also far over-diagnosed in America. Teachers recommend getting hyper kids evaluated, the doctors try Adderall to see if it helps, and sure enough it does. He sits still quietly and everyone's happy. But outside of North America people don't take kids to doctors and get experimental medications as the **first line of defense.** In America doctors say "let's try x medication and see if it helps." But in Europe medication is the last resort.

Teachers outside of America are much more comfortable with their authority, they're comfortable with using a **firm voice** to get a kid to stop doing disruptive behaviors.

Note – I recently learned of some students at a treatment school where there are both staff and teachers who help kids, that a teacher used a firm voice with misbehaving students, and the kids launched all manner of complains. Of course these days a licensed professional can get quickly fired for that sort of thing. The teacher asked the students why this was such an issue when the staff raise their voice at the kids all the time. The kids' response was that they were used to the staff raising their voice at the kids, but not the teachers. This shows that some populations won't respond to anything less, and it shows that when there is a norm, kids will respect that norm. It also shows one of the many double standards people insist on. Clearly proper limit setting and administration of consequences can eliminate much of the need for raising the voice, but there will always be kids who push the envelope and won't respond to minor corrections. When a leader can establish that they mean business the infractions and boundary testing typically dwindle if not entirely disappear, but a leader must be allowed to demonstrate that they mean to enforce their limits. Sometimes a firm voice to administer a small shock is entirely appropriate for this. We aren't calling for screaming insults at a child – it's the same as those who equate any physical discipline with  *'hitting.' Of course there is a spectrum, and extremes should be avoided on both ends as we effectively train youth.*

When a kid becomes reclusive, spending most of his time in video games, and becomes irritable from that behavior, parents are quick to take him to get a psychiatric diagnosis of ADHD and medicate him. Parents report the **sparkle** in the eye of a child going away once they get on these medications. When they get off the medication the sparkle comes back!

Sleep deprivation mimics ADHD almost perfectly. Many kids have gaming consoles in their bedrooms and their parents have no idea that they are staying up late gaming everyday.

Parents are compensating for sleep deprivation by powerful stimulation medications. Seroquel Conserta & Risperdal are being given to kids for these behaviors. A basic duty of a parent is to ensure the child gets enough sleep. *(Note - perhaps that's a good place to start using your parental authority & leadership. Make no mistake about it: to be a parent is to be a leader, and the most important sort.)* Now that we have online gaming popular at 2:00 a.m. and girls are staying up late on social media, parents need to be more assertive with their authority to say no. *(Note – many have a 'turn in your phone' curfew. If you want your kids to have these things at all, this is an essential limit to set.)*

In the US, around 10% of kids are on ADHD medication and in the UK it's about 0.7%. There's a 14x higher chance that an American kid will get treated with medication for ADHD than a kid in the UK. One family moved to America from England and they noticed a stark contrast - in America, all the teachers, doctors, everybody was pushing for her kids to get on ADHD medication!

From 2009 to 2013 there was a 10-fold increase in American ADHD diagnosis. Medicating kids under age 12 with mood stabilizers and antipsychotics between 1993-2009 went up 700%.
We have **turned misbehavior into a medical issue** to be diagnosed and medicated rather than trained and corrected. American parents are not doing their job of culturing kids!
Abdication of parental authority leads to prescription medication.

Note - If you won't train them, who will? No one has time for that, so then comes the pill… Sadly the big pharma brainwashing is so prevalent today that parents are forgetting their natural roles. One could say, we are on the brink of the extinction of parents… Aldous Huxley in his terrifying "Brave New World" book depicts a world where parents are not allowed to raise children. I wish that book were more fantastical than it is. The reality is that parents are the most qualified to train their children!

Note – A little thought here on homeschooling as it relates to parents passing on culture to their kids. My wife was planning with some other homeschool mothers in our community at a park recently, and a public school  *mom present was shocked by the entire concept of homeschooling. This shock is typical, as there are nice parents everywhere who have not been exposed to the idea. She wondered how the mothers schooled their children without licenses, and stated that she certainly wasn't qualified to school her kids. One of the moms piped up and encouraged this mother that as the parent of the child, she is the most qualified person to teach her child! This is right. Sure some community schooling can be appropriate, but we see a disturbing trend in thinking that the state knows better what the kids need than the parents.*

About 30 years ago the school principal, when there was a kid acting out, would have told the parent, "your son is rude, disrespectful, and exhibits no self-control. **You need to teach him some basic rules about civilized behavior if he is to stay at this school."** Now School administrators don't speak authoritatively to parents, they just suggest a medical practitioner or psychologist be consulted, at which point the kid is diagnosed with something and given medication.

Note – Ayn Rand in "Atlas Shrugged" points out that everyone these days is avoiding responsibility. We all have positions that we are afraid to take any action in. We live in a society of suing others, and walking on ice, hoping that the establishment won't throw us down. A world full of government grants, welfare spending, and high taxation toward a socialist state inevitably result in prizing position above action. We don't want to make waves. We don't want to build anything. We fear greatness. Well has it been said that fear is the number one tool of evil. Fear works upon people to freeze them, and keep them from doing good. And a good person who stops doing good is well, just a person. As Isaiah taught, the evil doers ways may appear unsurpassable, but in reality it is a mountain of chaff. We must not be afraid to have morals, and express them in the public world as we conduct our business.

When you tell a parent that their kid is disrespectful, responsibility is placed upon the parents to teach that kid. **With responsibility comes authority** to do something about the problem. But when a kid is instead referred for psychiatric evaluation, the **responsibility is transferred** to the physicians. Parents no longer ask what should we do to change his behavior, they ask whether their child should take medication.

ADHD medications all work in the same way - they increase dopamine, and it is very likely that long-term use of these medications results in a person being **unable to feel** normal feelings. If you do feel like you absolutely need a medication, try a **non-stimulant** one such as Startera, Intunive, or Wellbutrin. Antipsychotics traditionally used for treating schizophrenia are being used to treat kids' behaviors. Kids on these medications are much more likely to develop diabetes and obesity. The younger the child the greater the risk.

When kids have diagnoses the parents respond to their behaviors by saying '**he can't help it**, he has x diagnosis.' Of course the kids learn this too, and parrot the line, 'I can't help it, I have x.'
One boy ran around a classroom making buzzing noises and would not stop, ignoring the repeated instruction from the teacher. The teacher finally said "stop or else." The kid said "or else what?" The teacher said "or else I'll make you stop." The kid then buzzed even louder and

 the teacher tried to stop him at which point he bit her wrist drawing blood. The teacher called the parent and the parent said **"don't you know he has a psychiatric diagnosis**, he probably needs a medication change, you should have called the psychiatrist directly, don't you have his number?"

Note - This overmedicating of children is borderline child abuse. How ironic it is that people will be upset about a parent who is a little bit strict with their kid in training them, yet they're perfectly willing to throw the kid on some super toxic medication that could destroy his whole life in place of training. We are calling good evil and evil good.

Note – I see that one reason we are giving in to abdicating parental authority and turning to professionals and legalized drugs is that pastors are blending in with the socialist state in preaching a watered down grace-based theology, insisting that individuals should have minimal responsibility, and something big like a state or a god will take care of everything. The restored gospel message is that God's grace gives us power to act. Grace is not a get-out-of-responsibility card. It is a power that helps us to actually accomplish God's high standards. It is good news indeed when we learn that we can take our children back, and build a high and holy culture of light and truth like the ancients.

When teachers and parents **expect** good behavior, kids often give it. Command, don't ask, don't negotiate. The fact that a parent feels the need to negotiate already undermines their authority. When you lay down a rule and the kid asks why, the answer is **because mom / dad says so.** American parents two generations ago did this routinely and comfortably. Most British and Australian parents still do.

Doing a check up on a 6-year-old's sore throat, he said "now we're going to look at your throat." The parent interjected a question, "can the doctor look at your throat? We could get ice cream." **The parent turned it into a negotiation** and offered a bribe when it should have just been a task that quickly got done. The authority of the grown-ups was undermined. The situation unnecessarily became a long drawn out drama episode because when it was up to the kid, no, they didn't want the doc to look at their sore throat!

Older children can get more explanations, but younger children in particular should be commanded to do things. And these explanations are **not negotiations!** It's okay if the kid disagrees or doesn't see things your way.
The general rule for authoritative just right parents is "don't ask, command." The parents most horrified of the suggestion to command their kids are most likely to be medicating them! *(Because things will get out of control so quickly when you abdicate your leadership in the home! Something has to fill the vacuum to establish order if you don't!)*

Note – the way 'just right' parenting is described in the academic world these days is as follows, based on a continuum of love and expectations:
Low love + low expectations = neglect.
Low love + high expectations = authoritarian
High love + low expectations = permissive
High love + high expectations = authoritative (just right)

Parenting Types	High Expectations	Low Expectations
High Love	Authoritative (just right)	Permissive
Low Love	Authoritarian	Neglect

The words 'authoritarian' and 'authoritative' are too similar, but other than that it's a great way to understand this.

Note – there is a time and a place for making some rather sharp interventions. The D&C 121 helps us put the guardrails on this area of parenting where the tendency is to take it too far: "41 No power or influence can or ought to be maintained by virtue of the priesthood, only by persuasion, by long-suffering, by gentleness and meekness, and by love unfeigned; 42 By kindness, and pure knowledge, which shall greatly enlarge the soul without hypocrisy, and without guile—43 Reproving betimes with sharpness, when moved upon by the Holy Ghost; and then showing forth afterwards an increase of love toward him whom thou hast reproved, lest he esteem thee to be his enemy; 44 That he may know that thy faithfulness is stronger than the cords of death. 45 Let thy bowels also be full of charity towards all men, and to the household of faith, and let virtue garnish thy thoughts unceasingly; then shall thy confidence wax strong in the presence of God; and the doctrine of the priesthood shall distil upon thy soul as the dews from heaven. 46 The Holy Ghost shall be thy constant companion, and thy scepter an unchanging scepter of righteousness and truth; and thy dominion shall be an everlasting dominion, and without *compulsory means it shall flow unto thee forever and ever."*

Note – Kids should be taught a sense of duty to obey parents, and contribute to the family. A related topic here is allowance, kids wanting a regular welfare check for existing. Even when kids want an allowance for doing chores, this is something I caution against. Again, children must see their role in the family not as a privileged outside who needs payment, but as a member of the group who is expected to contribute to it. When allowances begin, they quickly inflate and the child learns an entitled attitude, like they can't lift a finger to help their own group without money. A love for money quickly dominates over the love for family you are trying to instill in them. When a child complains about not being paid for a chore, I like to point to the ceiling and remind them that they are getting a roof over their head, food, and so on. As a people aiming at Zion, I believe we need to learn to contribute to the group we belong to. All of the child's needs are met by the parents, they have no need for money. A child with lavish funds to spend on themselves is neither realistic, healthy, or of the spirit of Zion.

The family meal is a marker for a constellation of behaviors. Parents who eat with their kids are more likely to control the amount of video games, internet usage etc. a child has access to. No phones or TV ought be allowed in the background during family meals. In Scotland, Switzerland and New Zealand, it is less common than in America for families to have radio and TV on during dinner. Kids who have more meals with parents are less likely to feel sad, anxious and lonely, and are more likely to report feeling satisfied in life. They're less likely to have external problems such as fighting and skipping school. They're less likely to become obese later in life. **On a scale from 0 to 7 dinners with parents a week, the more dinners with parents the better off the kid was.** The change was statistically significant at almost every step. Kids with six dinners do better than those with five, etc. Parents around the world (but especially in America) mistakenly think that kids' time in dance and sports etc. is more important than time with the family around the dinner table.

When you get a report of bad behavior of your kid, don't rush to the child psychiatrist, talk to your kid. Parents are the ones with the primary responsibility for a kid to teach and enforce the rules of good behavior.

Note- perhaps over diagnoses and prescription by American doctors also has something to do with American doctors going into medicine for the prestige and money rather than for a genuine interest in helping people. It also surely represents uncritical thinking on behalf of these doctors. So they have seen a trend in aspiring young doctors and nurses who care less about people and are just getting a degree and a comfortable job.

Ch. 4 Why are American Students Falling Behind

Australian teachers don't have students undermining their authority, trying to bring them down. They do not have the culture of disrespect we do in America. Students in Australia routinely thank and praise their teachers.

Note - Shortly after reading this, I ran into a missionary from Australia. I told her about what I'd learned about the culture of disrespect in America, and how it isn't like that in Australia. She said "...well... yeah."

Even elite schools serving affluent kids in America have disruptive uninvolved rude boys and girls. Some think that the disrespect of the kids in America is the price we pay for greater creativity. *(Note – this sounds like Kamala Harris' socialist claim that high gas prices are the price we pay for democracy! These are not correct principles.)* But since 1995 American innovation has been remarkably narrow. Innovative leaders are now mostly in Europe and Asia. America is 11th in the world for filing patents per capita. 1945-1970 was the Golden era for American invention back when students were much more respectful and differential toward teachers.

(Note – while leftists reject the idea that America ever was great since it was never fully socialist, it is a fact that several elements of American greatness have been lost. Many know intuitively if by no other measurement, that there is a need to 'make America great again.' We

live in an apocalyptic society where the entire concepts of right and wrong are being erased. Satan is taking his throne incrementally, hiding in plain sight.)

Studies show that kids' creativity in America has gone down dramatically over the past two decades. We are seeing less synthesizing, less creativity, less energy, less  emotional expression, let's talkativeness, less verbal expression, less humorous, less imaginative, less unconventional, less lively and passionate, less perceptive, less apt to connect seemingly irrelevant things, and less likely to see things from a different angle.

The **culture of disrespect undermines true creativity** while strengthening same age **peer conformism.** There is nothing creative about a teenager telling an adult to shut up.

Even in the 1960s it was only a very small portion of students involved in the Vietnam War protests at schools.

Note- this is correct, and the book "The Politically Incorrect Guide to the 60s" by Jonathan Leaf goes into detail about this. (See my book highlights on it.) The 60s were a conservative time, but certainly a transition time. The loud minority found out how to take over the universities, etc.

In the book "The Smartest Kids in The World and How They Got That Way" by Amanda Ripley, it is demonstrated that America over invests in technology for education. The most successful countries are **utilitarian with no tech gadgets** in schools. The kids don't have wireless clickers and the board on the wall is only connected to the wall. Most kids just raise their hands and that works out fine. In America school sports trump academics; outside the US athletes are not excused from class to participate in games.

In America we try to make education cool and fun with screens and gadgets to motivate kids to learn, but the **solution is in changing the culture so students are less worried about pleasing peers.**

Teacher training in Finland is highly selective. It's as prestigious as getting into a medical school in the US. At some US colleges  students need higher academic standards to play football than to be a teacher.

American students who enroll in college are less likely than students in other countries to graduate. American students are studying less at college and learning less at college than a generation ago. They show little gains in cognitive skill, reasoning and critical thinking; only about a third of them go up more than one point on a 100-point scale during their college. They see college now more as building a social network than the pursuit of intellect. In the 60s American college students studied

25 hours a week, in the early 2000s it decreased to about 12 hours. American college students study less than college students anywhere in Europe with the exception of Slovakia. American graduates look mediocre or worse compared to graduates in other countries.

Note- with the trend in grading on effort rather than performance/merit, America is steadily going down. We are making an education inflation bubble to cover our poor teaching by lowering expectations so we can keep saying we are doing awesome. Eventually the bubble pops, everyone learns that the emperor has no clothes, that the whole thing has been a sham for decades. When the mark of the educated man is a hearty sense of socialism and entitlement, you know society won't last long.

Contemporary American culture and its pop music undermine academic scholarship. Kids outside of America spend more time doing homework and less time defending drag shows.

It's no longer true that a kid will get a good education just because he's in a good neighborhood. Parents must be extra involved to ensure their kids measure up not to American academic standards, but international.

Note – the best neighborhood you can find is a righteous one. Don't look for a rich one, they have their share of problems. How hardly can a rich man enter the kingdom of heaven said the Master. Now good like finding such a community.

Ch. 5 Why Are Kids So Fragile Today

Gamer kids are often out of shape and quick to give up at anything physically rigorous. More and more kids are aspiring to be professional video game players and **parents are afraid to deter** them from that dream. When the bubble of their amazing self-image popped, they are lost. The **online world creates an alternative culture dominated by mostly younger people**. Back in the day you heard stories of kids who tried out and failed but worked hard and came back and did great; you're not hearing those stories as much anymore. In the video game world the games come first - they are more important than family or health. If a gamer told his peers he was going to get in shape, they would think he is joking. Success in the real world means nothing to them.

Kids who do well in school encounter one difficult class and give up altogether. They need to learn the humility that comes with pushing through something hard, which they might not get perfect scores on for once.

Psychiatrists spend minimal time with a person before they prescribe dangerous medications. There is an extraordinary rise in the amount of youth in America being diagnosed with anxiety and depression.

Americans used to be at the top of the list for entrepreneurs and people actively looking for work, but now they're near the bottom. The rise in adults unemployed not looking for jobs more is pronounced in America than Europe.

A good parent-child relationship is robust and unconditional. Even when there are occasional problems and consequences the relationship remains intact. **But in peer relations everything is conditional** and contingent, leaving kids to be **anxious** about immediately answering texts from their friends etc. They don't want to look incompetent in front of their friends so they won't take risks to try to develop new skills. Children do need unconditional love and acceptance but that can't come from peers or a report card.

Schedule family **vacations** just for the family. **No friends** allowed or all that time your child will just be spent bonding  to the friend as an expensive play date. The main purpose of a family vacation is to strengthen the bonds between parent and child (and siblings). Strengthen bonds with children by going on walks, drives etc. on a weekly basis. Find edifying leisure activities like prayer, music, art and dance. Parent-child bonding needs to be a higher priority than extracurriculars or peer activities. Try to live near extended family to give your child more perspectives and connect them to your culture.

Note- this can also mean living in an area that has similar values. In the 2023 October General Conference, it was emphasized that we should stand with holy people in holy places. Good luck with that. But at least try.

Ultimately you only have control over your own household, so focus on that. But some areas are likely better than others. Here's a hint: the bible called for smaller towns where people actually have a name and a role. Of course, even the small towns today aren't interdependent, only the Amish have managed that. So good luck.

Your parenting style must change as your kid grows up. Of course, the newborn needs pure and constant affection. For a toddler your role is a cheerleader/encourager. As the kid gets older you must correct, redirect, and point out shortcomings.

If your teen can't think of anything fun to do other than gaming *(or social media, or wasting time with friends, etc.)*, shut down the game and get him into the real *(responsible, cultured)* world. Parents have the duty to instill their values upon their kids rather than just letting the world impress its values on them. The Internet and mobile phone are the **primary ways contemporary American culture is pushed** on to kids. The more time a kid spends with friends on the phone, the more likely they are to turn to peers rather than parents for guidance. These devices are **widening the generation gap** and undermine parental authority.

The more time kids spend on Instagram the more likely they are to think that Instagram is important. They become persuaded that their peers know about what's important and their parents don't.

In Holland schools close at noon every Wednesday so kids can have family time mid-week. In Geneva

Switzerland the schools close at lunch for two hours a day so kids can go home and have lunch with a parent. Employers often give extra time off work for people to go home and eat lunch with their kids. In Scotland's airport there are playgrounds etc. to accommodate their family friendly culture. In America there is **no institutional family time** built in, so you must fight for it. You have to cancel the extracurriculars, etc. Your kids **can't attach** to you if they hardly ever see you.

Note – the restored church called for Monday evenings to be set aside for family time, but even this is just to get the ball rolling. Any way we can return to a family-based society is the will of God. Family business. Home school. Choosing a family friendly faith filled community rather than the random public school community as the basis for peer friendships. Family work projects. Home grown food. Small multi-family group gatherings (as opposed to youth running around by themselves). Parent approved courting. Down time at home to just relax. Choosing from pre-approved family favorite movies rather than surfing the TV for the new show. Smaller homes so the family spends more time near one another. Larger sibling groups so the play group automatically has the same expectations. Parents not over working to keep up with the Jones.' Kids helping in research projects the parents are involved in. Older siblings participating in the teaching of younger siblings. Learning songs from a family songbook. Limiting peer play time to rare, structured events. Family service projects. Wholesome family recreation. Etc.

The waning of adult authority is directly related to the waning of attachment to adults, which is replaced with attachment to peers. An acorn shell prevents the seed from growing until the time is right, and if it's **prematurely opened, it won't grow** into a tree. A child whose primary attachment is to parents will become a successful (and balanced) adult, but **breaking generational bonds makes kids fragile.**

Part 2: Solutions

Ch. 6 What Matters

Self-control has now proven to be more important than openness to new ideas, friendliness, IQ, and GPA to predict whether an 11-year-old will be successful and happy 20 years later.

Many parents assume that good grades and test scores are the best predictors to happiness and achievement, but honestly integrity and self-control matter much more. People who are more **conscientious (having self-control & integrity)** earn and save more money, are happier and more satisfied with life, are less likely to be obese, are more likely to live longer, and are less likely to abuse substances and engage in risky sexual behaviors. **No other personality (character) trait has this strong of a correlation**.

Note- at the heart of being conscientious is self-discipline and a moral compass guided by conscious and strict training.

Going to bed early and getting up early are good measures of deliberate self-control. Self-control is the characteristic most emblematic of conscientiousness. Parents must set the example of self-control by avoiding late night indulgences and keeping their word.

Note – sometimes parents should burn the midnight oil, but in useful matters, not binge watching of shows. Even if your schedule isn't always early to bed early to rise, make it clear that you are on a mission, and that nothing could be more rewarding! And yes, the early bed and early rise works well for most people. Most of the extremely late nights and extremely late mornings aren't from doing useful things…

Note – everyone needs to find a mission. This goes beyond formal church callings. Find what you're good at, something that makes you come alive which makes the world that much more beautiful and wonderful, then enjoy wearing out your life to magnify that calling which the holy spirit has given you. Obviously these callings will not contradict basic Christian standards.

Note- yes, kids hold onto every word, do your best to follow through on even the small commitments. Kids understand maybe to mean yes, so be careful with that. And it's not only the youth these days who have trouble with excessive technology usage – let's admit that we are whipped by these surprisingly addictive time wasters, and find solutions for all.

People who make lots of money can still be in financial distress when they don't know how to live within their means. People with a low IQ can succeed due to discipline, and people with high IQ without discipline often fail.

You help an 8-year-old build self-control by saying no dessert till you eat your vegetables. You help a teenager build self-control by saying no electronics until after homework.

In a matter of weeks, a child can change from being impulsive to self-controlled with the correct behavior intervention. If you're going to change the rules, tell your children that you're going to and why. After 6 weeks of consistent enforcement of rules your child will be more respectful to you and other adults. This increased structure will result in both the parent and child **enjoying life more**.

Note- this is a great key, when we train our kids, they actually become more enjoyable. Many parents today complain of not enjoying parenting, and it is likely connected to their letting their kids treat them as doormats and butlers. Even if there are some hard times of establishing that you really mean business, once the parameters are set and the bluffs are called out, things stabilize, and a structure of safety and peace for all ensues. Well trained children are set up for a lifetime of success, social acceptance, and joy. Parents who discipline their kids correctly and consistently soon find that such discipline is hardly, if ever, needed. The critics complain that these are 'short term' results only, but the fact is that kids need to learn good behavior, and when they have the experience of good behavior, the spirit will reward them with joy for that, so they'll know by their experience that 1. They are capable of good behavior and 2. That it is in their best interest to behave.

Note – I remember in a classroom once, there were some students misbehaving badly. I had to crack down on the rules and structure of the class. This transition time for them was hard for us all. A student said, "I don't even like this class." I responded, "Neither do I." It shocked the student to see that it goes both ways. I taught them that the only way anyone will enjoy the class is when good behavior prevails.

Parenting is not about teaching cliches like "follow your dreams." Help them see which dreams aren't realistic, because no one else will.

Note - Parental training is more about teaching kids to say "ok" to a parent than getting a straight A in a class or excelling on a football team. It's been said that sports build character, the more likely reality is that sports reveal character (otherwise all athletes would be pinnacles of virtue...) No, we aren't just teaching not mindless compliance, we're teaching knowledge of how to work and thrive within structured systems, which are a big part of real life. If you can't figure that out everyone is going to hate you.

Researcher Carol Dweck suggests never telling your kids they are smart, but praising them for working hard so they don't give up the first time they don't already know an answer to a problem. *(Note – you can teach a kid they're smart if you define smart as someone who works hard to figure things out.)* Interestingly **when it comes to teaching virtue, praising identity works better than praising behavior.** For example, it's better to say "I can see you're a very kind person" than "that's a very kind thing you did." In one study participants were told the study was to find the prevalence of "cheating" and in another they were told to study was to find the prevalence of "cheaters." Cheating more than doubled when they just said they were looking for cheating rather than for cheaters. **Apparently kids are more comfortable cheating if they don't see themselves as cheaters.** Similarly kids are more likely to help in a project if they are encouraged to be **helpers rather than just to help**.

Note- they learn 'this is who I am, therefore, this is what I do!' This is also why it is so critical to learn (and endorse) one's identity as children of God. 'I'm a Christian, so this is what I do!'

Many students report having high ethics yet they also admit cheating. They are separating cheating from ethical behavior. They see themselves as nice kids who occasionally cheat, not as cheaters. In reality **behavior influences and eventually becomes identity.** If you cheat over and over you are or will soon become a cheater! Your actions over time will change your character. Parents used to teach these **moral fundamentals** but many no longer do.

*Note- this is a very important point. There's a big trend now to only identify behaviors and fail to identify the negative identity character traits that those behaviors turn a person into. As the popular saying goes, 'you made a bad choice, you're not a bad person.' This is often polite and sometimes encouraging, but it's not the whole truth. If you consistently make bad choices, you are in fact a bad person, and that used to be common knowledge. The recent advent of **refusal to connect behavior with identity** is destructive.*

Note – Connecting behavior with identity does not mean go around pointing fingers, it means when you have to, tell it like it is. It means teach true doctrine, not watered-down feel-good euphemisms. Obviously, everyone needs to be reminded that they are children of God with lots of potential; but they also need reality checks. 2 Nephi 9 of the Book of Mormon makes it clear that liars go to hell - not just people who lie, but liars.

Note - The good news of the gospel is that Christ can grant us a return to innocence, but for those who reject goodness, there's also bad news. Of course, we emphasize the good news, but if we entirely seek to delete the bad news, then the good news becomes fake and meaningless. The bad news is the inevitable Shakespearian tragedy life becomes without Christ. It's like how the atonement isn't important to people who don't understand the fall. The doctrine of the fall is that we are broken and in desperate need of help. When someone understands this and isn't overly pumped full of self esteem, they can more readily accept the need for atonement in their life.

Note - It's like how without justice and law, there can be no mercy. This is also central for the entire foundation of Christianity: that God upholds justice, and the only chance we've got is if a 3rd party savior intervenes on our behalf. Why a 3rd party and not God himself? Because then mercy would rob justice, and an unjust God would cease to be God. The Book of Mormon teaches these foundations of Christian philosophy better than any other book.

Note - Catholic Philosophy professor Peter Kreeft in his epic book "How to Win the Culture War" (see my notes on his book) points out that because we love the person, we hate the sin. Often people want to identify with their sin and say their sin is a normal part of them which we must accept (especially the sin of homosexuality). But Christians know that each person is inherently valuable, so we want to cure them of the cancer, which is the sin (or character flaw). Loving someone requires that you call them out on the problem, not support them in it. So no, we aren't just going with 'that's just who I am' as a justification for undeveloped character. We know better. That's not who you are. The most fundamental 'you' is not your sin; it is your divine parentage.

Over the past two decades the ethics of students have gone way down. They want to be successful and they think their colleagues are cheating, so they cheat to compete. "Just do it" and "go for it" define popular American culture, with Pepsi billboards saying, "live for now." This *directionless immoral impulsive animalistic* philosophy is a symptom of the collapse of parenting.

One kid had a promising career in football, but his father told him, "you'll be spending this summer on a fishing boat." He didn't ask, he told. The father didn't say anything, he just signed his son up for a tough summer job. At the time the son resented it, but he later appreciated it as a time where he learned hard work and empathy for what others' difficult lives are like.

You don't teach virtue by teaching, you teach it by requiring virtuous behavior so that virtuous behavior becomes a habit. There is a popular notion that if you want a kid to be virtuous you first have to explain to them the benefit of being virtuous. But virtuous behavior is what causes people to become virtuous. If you compel children to act more virtuously, they actually become more virtuous. **Proverbs** says train up a child in the way he should go and when he is old he will not depart from it. If you compel a child to behave virtuously, when he is an adult he will continue to behave virtuously. Aristotle wrote that a person becomes virtuous by **repeatedly practicing** virtue. Excellence is not an act, but a habit.

Note – again, Peter Kreef has useful material on this in Culture War, that we have to focus more on doing than planning (and teaching). The restoration has had a strong theme of doing as well. If all we do is preach, we won't have built anything, and there's no salvation in that.

Many parents think they need to let their kids do whatever they want, to spend hours on games, to stay up late photo-shopping selfies for Instagram, and texting. Parents now think that kids can grow up doing whatever they want and **suddenly become virtuous** when they are adults.

Note – one important example is that if we train a child to have work ethic via chores and other rigorous expectations, that child will be empowered with the character trait of hard work, which can then transfer into the classroom, the workplace, etc., and enable them to excel in life.

The Hebrew of Deuteronomy doesn't say "**teach** [the law] diligently" to children, it says "**inscribe** them on your children." The Hebrew verb used here is "shanon" meaning to **cut** with a knife. To say merely "teach them diligently" is watered down.

Note – this sounds like something a little beyond brief nightly family scripture readings and the Sunday trip to the church house.

You must ask kids to **pretend that they are virtuous** before they really are. Action shapes character. CS Lewis said that the **pretense leads to the real** thing. When you are not feeling particularly friendly, behave as though you are, and a few minutes later you will be. To get a quality you must begin to behave as though you have it. This is often the only way to get good habits. *(Note – act well, dress well, talk well, work well, and you're well on your way to virtue.)*

Many college graduates go to Wall Street not knowing what to do with their lives, thinking, 'if you don't know what to do, you may as well make money.' They fail to realize that the environment of **money seeking impacts** a person's character.

The 21st century assumption is that if you give kids a choice between right and wrong and show them why they should choose right, that they will **choose right on their own**. This is a mere guess about human nature which **evidence does not support.**  Rather than giving kids the option of healthy and unhealthy lunch, require them to eat the healthy lunch for years, then they will have learned the benefits and habits of that character.

The **ideal of education** is not to learn a bunch of things, it's **to learn culture.** When kids aren't cultured they have no standard to measure pop culture against. They don't know that today's music is garbage because they **haven't seen the real good stuff**. They don't know that porn masturbation and video games are just **cheap substitutes** for what life really has to offer. They don't know how to compare the virtuous lifestyle of Mother Teresa to the selfish lifestyle of popular figures.

Self-control and honesty are **not innate**; they must be taught. You can't rely on US schools today to do this job. Some people call abdicating parental authority as 'enlightened wisdom,' but it is neither. It is a mere retreat from adult responsibility.

Note- Ayn Rand (despite her obvious flaws which Dr. Sax has pointed out,) does a good job depicting some of this in her books - that there are fewer and fewer people willing to take responsibility, willing to act, willing to make decisions, and more people who simply refer you to someone else to solve the problem. What is life if we never take the blame, good or bad? People are no longer willing to risk, and are living shell lives, ever hiding behind the next bigger bloke. Of course, one area of great risk we must all take is family life. At some point we have to take the step of marriage and parenting, and give it our best shot. It's better to have loved and lost than to never have loved at all! It's the same with school, work etc. - just do something! Trust your instincts! Don't let decades go by just spinning your wheels! When we take steps forward in the direction we think we should, it almost always teaches us the lessons we need to learn. Jesus talks about this when he says he would rather us be hot or cold, not lukewarm. When we are people of action, God can, by and by, redirect our action in a higher way; but when we are people of inaction, God can't do much with that.

Ch. 7 Misconceptions

People think if they prevent their kids from doing stuff they want to do, they will be **crazy as soon as they leave the house**, having 'not learned how to choose good behavior on their own.' But **longitudinal studies show that well behaved kids are more likely to grow up to be well behaved adults**. Kids raised by more **permissive** parents are **more likely to get in trouble as**

adults. People who think kids who grow up in strict homes will become wild adults are often basing that on some popular movie or something Oprah said. Research provides no support for this notion and flatly contradicts it! If you're hiring a new employee and one candidate has a track record of honesty and hard work whereas the other has a track record of idleness and troublemaking, which will you hire? The same logic applies with how we treat kids and what kind of adults they'll turn into. Parents used to understand this.

The line of what is a child and what is an adult isn't so clear as the legal age makes it seem - no magic transfer of responsibility takes place on the 18th birthday. *(Note – it seems pretty clear that we are stalling too long to teach youths responsibility. We've all seen the lazy untrained 18-year-old, and the excellent mature 18-year-old. Church missions and military service can help young adults catch up in maturation, but even in these areas you can tell who had good training and who*

68

*didn't. These differences also make the age for marriage
readiness differ from person to person.)*

There's too hard, too soft, and just right. Too hard
parents rarely show any love and have excessive
demands. Parents that are too soft don't have rules and
consequences. If you are not enforcing rules, you are too
soft. Just right parents show love and have consistent
rules. Just right means being both strict and loving.
The public understanding over the past 30 years of what
it means to be a just right parent has **drifted steadily**
away from **authoritative to permissive**. Parents don't
have to choose between being strict or loving.

Note – remember the chart from earlier:

Parenting Types	High Expectations	Low Expectations
High Love	*Authoritative (just right)*	*Permissive*
Low Love	*Authoritarian*	*Neglect*

Parents worry that if they are strict their child will be an
outcast, the only one not allowed to do what others are
doing. Often the kids are fine with a peer not having a
phone etc., it's the parents who are the most concerned.

*Note – peer pressure doesn't stop when you become an
adult! The village will let you know if they approve of
your methods! Of course in some ways this is helpful,
but in our permissive backward society, you often have
to be willing to stand against the crowd, and you can, in
the sanctuary of your home.*

69

See Books by Meg Meeker:
Strong Fathers, Strong Daughters: 10 Secrets Every
Father Should Know
And
Strong Mothers, Strong Sons: Lessons Mothers Need to
Raise Extraordinary Men

Author Meg Meeker didn't let her son play video games.
Her son insisted that when he was an adult living on his
own, he would get some video games and be like the
other guys. He did so but ended up selling them as they
only collected dust. As a youth he didn't **identify** as a
gamer, his identity involved people skills and various
cultured interests and hobbies. He was not **impressed** by
video game skills as he matured. He observed that
gamers were often clumsy in real life situations. **Age
matters**. If a boy starts playing **games as a young
person they will imprint** on his brain in a way that they
won't when he is 18. The young brain is very plastic and
immature.

*Note - great point, we must make limits on the minors we
are responsible for so that they become balanced adults.
Without limits as children, people can develop toxic
addictions from warped culture which last through life.
Kids depend on adults to help guide them.*

Longitudinal studies show that kids who spend many
hours a week playing **violent video games** become more
hostile, less honest and less kind. This is the impact of
years of playing those games. **Ban** first person shooter
games from the house. If your kids like shooting things

let them go to a **gun club** and really shoot things. If your child's friend plays violent video games **do not allow him to go to that house**.

It is **not important for your children to be popular**. Being popular in the US today often entails **unhealthy behavior and attitudes** beginning with a disregard for parental authority.
Being kind and self-controlled is what matters.

Note – one of my key issues with the public schools are the prevalent attitudes there. Those are almost impossible to shake. We can sometimes make up for some false doctrines they teach (and yes they teach lots of those), but the attitudes of peers is likely the most toxic element. The anti-family messages of peer culture can shake the very foundation of your home.

It is realistic for you to hold your children responsible for their behavior. 'Just right' parents expect their children to **behave the same way out of the home** as they do in the home. That's integrity. Parents can drop by a friend's house to see what the kids are doing unannounced, etc.

Some parents **don't give their children a phone at all even through High School** as there's no need for it. The other peers don't really care, it's the other parents who get on your case. Parents peer pressure other parents to give kids phones.

Note- this is great counsel - if a kid needs to make a phone call for something they can borrow the parents phone. But the big picture is that phones are much less needed than people think, particularly for youth. These are the source of most of youths troubles these days, and the positives they offer can easily be offered by limited windows of checking out an electronic device from a parent to use some educational planned program or website.

It is **never acceptable for your child to be disrespectful to you**. It's okay for a kid to say 'I don't agree with you' but it's never okay for a kid to say 'shut up'. Don't allow that language in your house. *(Note – not allowing something means teaching them why it's not ok, setting the expectation that such won't be allowed, reminding them as needed, and giving consequences if the behavior continues.)*

Show kids that people can disagree respectfully. Disagree about something on casual to practice so they can respectfully disagree on more important topics without disliking the other person. Listen to each other and state why your opinion is different.

Many parents don't want to interfere with what supposedly makes their kid happy. But this is **confusing happiness with pleasure**. *(Note – surely unrestrained pleasure will destroy anyone.)* Many kids value the virtual world of video games and relationships in that virtual world more than real world abilities and relationships. The **gaming world** may give them pleasure but it will not give them sustained lasting happiness. Pleasure often transforms into addiction. The hallmark of addiction is decreasing pleasure over time.

Tolerance develops and the game becomes impulsive, involuntary and un-thrilling; the addict cannot find pleasure in anything else. **Happiness comes from fulfilling your potential, which is beyond online gaming**. Parents concerned about their children's gaming should **follow their instincts and intervene** even if the kid claims they can make a living off it and have friends from it. **The desire to live in the virtual world is an uneducated desire.** It isn't easy to intervene but you're not trying to win your kids approval, you're trying to **do your job as a parent, to help your child find their potential.** You may not know precisely where your child's potential is but it's surely not in 20 hours a week online gaming. The same applies to limiting social media and texting.

The **job of a parent is to teach a child to enjoy things that are higher** than cotton candy. Video games, Instagram and texting are the cotton candy of today's pop culture. Parents must battle the culture of 'live for now' and to teach in its place integrity. Today's cultural message is that your child is fulfilled when he gets what he desires. *(Note – just look at what has happened to Christmas.)* Pop culture says a child knows how to be fulfilled better than parents' instincts. The popular message today is 'do whatever feels good, whatever floats your boat' *(you do you, follow your truth).*

Note- this is like the slogan of the Rolling Stones which they adopted from Satanist leader Allester Crowley, "Do as thou wilt, this is the whole of the law." (PS- the Beatles praised this guy and featured on an album cover, calling him a 'lonely heart.' No, his is an evil heart! Guess what, it's ok to say that! It's called the truth.)

Arthur C Brooks pointed out that today's goal of 'if it feels good do it' **equates our morals with protozoa.** Living just for the present is the culture of infants. **Being a human means** more than gratification of immediate desires. It involves service, mastery of the arts, faith in something greater than oneself, discipline in pursuit of a higher goal.

Is false that to love someone you must trust them. Just because you love your child doesn't mean you have to believe they're always telling the truth. Adult relationships do involve more trust, but parent-child relationships are different from marriage relationships. Parents who think their child will never lie to them are wrong. Your children are more likely to lie to you than anyone else because they don't want to let you down. Though cheating is viewed casually today, they have a feeling that their parents' morals of no cheating is correct, so they are very likely to lie to their parents about cheating.

Note - other popular activities youth hide from parents include sloppy dress, foul language, inappropriate premature dating and intimate relations, movies watched with peers, skipping class, skipping homework, drug use, pornography use, etc.

A generation ago there was an alliance between parents and schools. If kids cheated in school parents would be notified and give consequences to reinforce the school discipline. Today when the school tries to punish a kid, the parents often oppose it.

Note - It's not just parents who think the teachers are being too strict – more often what I've seen is that the schools are overly permissive and therefore not supporting the parents mission. If this is the case for you and that alliance is no longer working, is it still wise to send your kids there? We live in the Great age of homeschooling. Thousands woke up to this during Covid. Likely homeschooling will be illegal before long as government power expands (they're already shutting it down in some countries), but the tools and reason to homeschool now are greater than ever.

One schoolteacher reprimanded a kid for cheating on a test in front of the class. The kids' parents had friends on the school board and were wealthy donors, so they made some phone calls and the teacher was informed that if she didn't want to lose her job she needed to apologize to the girl in front of the whole class. So the teacher did so, and told the class 'the district doesn't care if you cheat, if you do so, I won't say a word.'

Note- good for her at least trying to expose the corruption of the district. More and more organizations are chasing out all the honest people with their dishonest policies.

Note- There is a new trend now for school administrators to get rid of tests in general! There isn't a point of a test where the students are allowed to use whatever resources they want. At that point it's no longer a test, it's no longer demonstrating what you know. It wipes out the integrity of the entire classroom. It trades education for cheap tricks. Eliminating tests only further enables kids to waste class time. Whatever the grandiose theory behind eliminating tests is, the reality is that it encourages idleness. It's like communism, it may sound nice, but it simply doesn't work in practice. The correctness of a theory is limited by how much it really works in practice. When someone says they don't do well on tests, it usually means they don't know the material. Elder David A Bednar recently taught that giving tests are very important in assessing progress. When we know where students are, we can know where to direct them. Now blackmailing kids' future prospects by a GPA which cannot be remediated, that's a whole different conversation.

Some parents fear that if they're strict with their kids, their kids won't love them anymore. But remember the job description of a parent. **The reward of a parent is knowing that you've done your job well. Merely seeking affection from your kids is not the top goal.** Often single parents are lonely and want excessive affection from their children and they trade their authority for this. In a relationship with an adult you are equals where everything is negotiable and you can't give orders. But the relationship with the child is different, you have to set the rules and enforce them even if the child doesn't agree. Kids need this!

The most common error in parenting is becoming too permissive out of a desire to win the affection of your kids.

Sometimes kids express hatred to their parents, and sometimes the parents aren't too fond of their misbehaving kids. But the parent must stand by their authority to say no when their gut tells them to. When misfortune befalls a kid, the parent often laments that **they knew** they should have avoided the situation, not allowed the activity etc., but they didn't. Even if you're concerned that doing your job as a parent will lose the affection of your child, you must do your job!

Ch. 8 Teach Humility

Parents say they want their kids to grow up to be kind and happy, but they don't know how to make that happen. They often **confuse achievement with fulfillment**. Many American parents have **confused virtue with success**. Humility is now an un-American virtue. They teach that the only real sin is failure.

People don't even know what humility means. They think it's saying you're stupid when you know you're smart. Humility means being as interested in others as you are yourself. It's listening to others and being

interested in their views.

(Note – and it's recognizing that God's ways are higher than your ways, that if your ideas contradict God's laws, they aren't something to entertain. It's knowing that no matter how far we have come, we still have a long way to go. Treating others well is easier when we remember where we came from, and how good God has been to us all the while.)

We often hear 'dream until your dreams come true.' A better slogan would be work until your dreams come true. Even better is to say 'work to pursue your dreams but realize that life is what happens on the way.' *(Note- and the best saying would be 'work to pursue God's will.')*

Often kids are assigned to write about how amazing they are.

High self-esteem at a young age sets a person up for disappointment and resentment at age 25. When parents and teachers carefully nurture self-esteem, it often results in a crash after college when they learn that just because everyone said they are amazing doesn't mean they are. A **culture of self-esteem leads to a culture of resentment, confusion and hostility** about people who actually do succeed. Courage involves recognizing risks and your own limitations. Humble people rejoice at the success of others.

Note – when youth are aware of not only their strengths but also their weaknesses, they can work to improve their weaknesses. This is surely a better path toward success than ignorantly going through life. This is also why we need to make them aware of both the strengths and weaknesses of various political policies, organizations, and even peers.

The protagonists in the works of Ayn Rand are unabashedly selfish. They pursue their own interests relentlessly and unapologetically. None of the major protagonists are parents, nor is the author. It is immature when you think the world is all about what you want.

Note- I don't think this is a totally correct representation of the heroes of Rand. Of course, he is right that they are too self-centered, but the heroes definitely have redeeming qualities even in this regard. They treat their employees with respect and equality based on merit.

They recognize the evils of forced redistribution of wealth, and even though they aren't themselves parents, they show many proper social governing dynamics in how they work with their peers and society. Interestingly Joseph Smith taught that self-aggrandizement is a true principle when you are doing God's work, in so much as the bigger you get the more you can help others. The question was put to him, "Joseph, is the principle of self-aggrandizement wrong? Should we seek our own good?" His answer: "It is a correct principle and may be indulged upon only one rule or plan-and that is to elevate, benefit, and bless others first. If you will elevate others, the very work itself will exalt you. Upon no other plan can a man justly and permanently aggrandize himself." (Truman Madsen Joseph Smith tapes) Consider God himself, if he had less power and

influence than he does, he would not be in the position he is to offer mercy and goodness to so many. I think the heroes of Rand ultimately would benefit the lives of their peers, but it is true that the heroes in the story do lack principles of chastity and religion and are more heroes of the terrestrial level than the celestial level.

When a kid has learned humility they are more likely to recognize whether they're trying to do something just to look good, or doing that thing because they are genuinely interested in it.

In an era of 'walk tall and stand proud' it takes courage to teach humility.

Note- yes, true humility is both empowering and a unique path in life these days. As the old saying goes, you may not be as high on the ladder, but you are climbing a more important ladder (or multiple ladders). People often won't recognize that and call you a fool. But your goals are completely different from their goals. For example, you might  *lose a soccer game because you value your teammates having fun so you pass the ball the less skilled player; you might be removed from an intensive program requiring perfect attendance because you had to help someone at a critical time; you might be a friend to someone who isn't particularly friendly because you're not in it for you but for them; you might make a lower wage because what you do during the day creates meaning in the lives of others; Naturally all of this must be done in wisdom and order, but remember, God's ways are higher than our ways; His wisdom and order may look different than the wisdom of others. As the saying goes, what on earth are you doing for heaven's sake?*

Many families require their kids to do **rigorous chores** even if friends are visiting and even if they have lots of homework. Many parents who can afford to hire out manual labor choose to have their kids do it to teach their kids the value of hard work. If it doesn't require an electric current, you can usually do it yourself with your family. It's a mistake to hire out all the manual chores so

81

your kid has more time for schoolwork and extracurriculars. You send an unintended message to your kids that they are too important to do menial tasks.

Teach kids that the world does not revolve around them. They are a member of a family with obligations to the family, and those obligations are paramount. One family did not allow their kid to go to an after ball game party because the ball game was the time for recreation, then it was time to go back to chores. Of course other parents judged them for this, but they were confident in their family vision. Again, peer pressure isn't just from kid to kid.

Teach your kids early on that they won't be the cool kid. For an American kid to be cool nowadays it means dressing provocatively, disrespecting your parents, and staying out late at night. Don't allow any of that.

Denzel Washington once came home proud of how he became a star. His mom rebuked him saying "you don't know how many people have been praying for you and for how long, go get a bucket and wash the windows."

"The culture of social media is the antithesis of humility." Social media as used by youth are all about self-promotion. It's all about broadcasting and aggrandizing the self.
Usually when a parent is trying to help a kid, but the **kid remains rude, the root cause is access to social media.** It's not about whether you should be your kid's friend on social media - if your kid is into the culture of disrespect, get them off the media!

Ch. 9 Enjoy

When was the last time you did something with your kid that you both totally enjoy?

American mothers spend more time on childcare but enjoy it less than French women. Most likely the French kids are better behaved. *(Note – and it's not luck of the draw...)*

It's no fun to try and field texts and emails while you're with your kid. When you're with your kid, focus on your kid.

Note – kids should be in every part of our lives, so yes you're going to have to do other things with them. But the point is to make time set aside to just focus on them. Many are so rushed that they feel they can't do this, and that's when a paradigm shift needs to happen, and certain things need to be eliminated.

Spend time together outdoors so you are not tempted to look at a screen. Kids may resist going on outings at first, but they enjoy it when you're there. Sometimes kids don't want to go have family fun and the parent has to say **"too bad you're going."** Once kids discover that they can have **fun with their parents the relationship totally changes.**

Spending fun time with your child is **not an optional elective** to be squeezed in after you've done the work of the day, it is essential. You must plan for it, insist on it, and make time for it. *(Note – similarly, some think that the arts of high culture are optional, but we are finding that these are as essential as anything else. Of course, fun time with kids should be based in high culture type recreation.)*

One successful college football player reported that during his senior year of high school, even though he was very successful and could have spent all his time at parties, his favorite pastime was to spend the evening at home with his parents.

He declined invitations to parties to stay home with his parents to play board games or watch old movies with them. His parents were both strict and loving. In this family the kids were **not allowed to play at a home where there were no parents**, and **dates had to be interviewed by the parents**, and dates were **not allowed into bedrooms**. The kids thought they would need therapy from all the terrible things their parents were doing to them (the rules), then the kids went to college and watched everyone else's lives fall apart, and realized that **it was everyone else that was going to need therapy.**

Little things make the best happiness. Simple family activities like a board game or a sport or an old movie.

(Note – little local events, not lavish vacations or expensive toys, are the foundation of family recreation.)

Absolutely no screens at dinner.

Vehicle entertainment systems show kids smiling in the back seat with headphones and the mother smiling. Its as though the mother is saying, "isn't this great, we can spend hours together and I don't have to talk to them at all!" Everyone is in a rush, take advantage of what time you have to talk, including the car. Don't allow your kid to separate themselves from you by putting on headphones in the car or any other time they are with you. *(Note – there are times when adult learning is separate from children's learning but beware of the tendency to over isolate.)*

It requires a significant investment of time to devote attention to kids. Adults and children may need to cut back on their schedules to get family time. Many parents and kids are simply trying to do too much. They send an **unintended message that relaxed time together as a family is the least important** thing in life. Many parents are overbooked and **instead of cutting back they overbooked their kids** so their kids can be as stressed and overwhelmed as they are.

Outside of America it's rare to find people who **boast about how busy** and sleep deprived they are. Americans complain about their busy lives are and often it's actually **boasting**. It's rare to find full-time parents outside of

America who spend all day **chauffeuring** kids around even over the summer holiday.

Parents need to **teach their kids balance, to not be over scheduled**. The joy of quiet moments. *(Note – beware the ever on television.)* When parents overly emphasize skills that the child can gain, they are sending an unintended message that 'what you do is more important than who you are,' **that achievements matter more than family.**

Note – we must realize that family life is the greatest achievement. We must be satisfied with the simple life of

basic goodness and contribution. We must avoid the siren call to be top professionals making top dollar, or fame, etc.

Don't push a kid to live as though they were continually preparing their college application (or job resume).
When kids learn to not worry about what they look like in the eyes of others they can do less and become more.

Note - to 'do less' isn't to say be a bum hippy. It is to say, less focus on trivial things and monetary things, and more focus on eternal things like relationships, spirituality, wisdom, and truth. More rest in ways that actually rejuvenate and uplift. As Hugh Nibley puts it, we all have a full-time job discovering the history of this world. We are a bunch of ignoramuses. But when you are chronically overscheduled with work, extracurriculars, fanciness or other trivialities, cutting things out of the schedule is a great place to start, and the only way you'll begin to have time for high culture, and wholesome (modest) recreation (which is an essential ingredient in family life).

You might have to **move to find a less stressful job or learn how to become comfortable on less income**. Parents must teach priorities; they **must teach the meaning of life!**

Note- The excuse is often made 'we have to provide' when what is really happening is endless toil to have the bigger house, the fancy clothes and beauty products, the elaborate vacations (when usually tossing a ball at home will suffice), etc. Both men and women must watch out for what they are doing, what they are asking each other to do, and keep a razor focus on the essentials, or we will miss it.

Ch. 10 The Meaning of Life

The middle-class script everyone in America repeats is:
1. Work hard in school so you can get into a good college.
2. Get into a college so you can get a good job.
3. Get a good job so you can make a good living and have a good life.

All of this is false! Here's the reality:

1. Working hard in school is no guarantee you'll get into a good college.
2. A good college is no guarantee of a good job. Many graduates are waiting tables or are unemployed.
3. Having a good job is no guarantee of having a good life.

In Germany and Switzerland there's **no shame** if a kid wants to become an **auto mechanic instead of**  **going to university,** even if both the parents are university professors. But in America there's a stigma attached to being a mechanic, a **lack of respect attached to blue collar work**.

Many American parents think the primary purpose of K-12 schooling is to get into an elite college. But K-12 should actually be to **prepare us for life, not more school.** Many of the skills needed for life are different from the skills needed for getting into a top university. Kids focused on college avoid classes that might be difficult since they might not get an 'A,' even if those classes interest them. They sign up for extracurriculars not because they're interesting but because they might look good on a resume. They aren't living, they are performing. Sadly parents encourage this performing.

Note- it's quite tragic that the graduate must know the various classes of worms (part of the biology required curriculum), but need not know anything of farming, astronomy, nutrition, construction, finance, and so forth. Schools can never teach it all, but we wish they would teach more practical things.

Young people choose to be doctors because it looks like a clear path to a fulfilling life. But these people often don't have basic things about life figured out. They don't know what they really want in life, what will really make them happy.

Note - maybe this is why they're just prescribing everyone medication, because they really don't know the answers!

There are many miserable wealthy people who work 80 hours a week and loath what they do. If you loath what you do you are a slave. Time is precious. No amount of money can recover lost time. This leads to resentment for what they do, such as doctors who resent their patients.

Note - On the one hand fathers are primarily responsible to provide, and that can mean a less preferred job. But insomuch as there are reasonable alternatives, and insomuch as we are often living for wealth rather than a faith-based approach to finance of meeting our basic needs and setting a little aside for times of trouble, to these extents we often can and should find more fulfilling work.

Note - All of this said, Mike Rowe of "Dirty Jobs" points out that people can learn to love even tough and seemingly menial jobs; when you get good at something, and take ownership of it, you can find lots of joy in it. One sewer worker on Mike's show said, after having worked in the sewer industry and becoming good at what he did, 'one day I woke up and realized, I'm passionate about people's crap!' Further, running your own business doing something others would consider trivial can be much more fulfilling than working for someone else.

Note- someone recently spoke to me that we are seeing Isaiah's times of rude youth, and so it is, but I say we cannot go on in such permissive management of them. The plague is of the authorities, not just the youth! The youth are likely the more innocent ones in this scenario. Each must chose whether they will hearken to the whisperings of conscience, or continue in the false traditions of their fathers. Wickedness is compounding across generations, and we have to own up to our part of it.

The middle-class script can make your kid more risk-averse and cautious, and that does not help him prepare for life. Willingness to fail is one of the keys to life, but it's not part of the script of getting perfect grades going to the perfect school and getting the perfect job, so they never take risks.

Note - they quickly learn to oppress all feelings not calculated to maximize profits. Is it a stretch to say they have sold their souls?

Empower your children to take risks and congratulate them not only when they succeed, but when they fail, because failure brings humility which can bring growth and wisdom and an openness to new things in a way that success almost never does.

Steve Jobs said getting fired from Apple *(which he helped found and to which he later returned)* was the best thing that could have happened to him. The heaviness of being successful was replaced by the lightness of being a beginner again, being less sure about everything, freeing him to enter one of the most creative periods of his life.

Note – Jordan Peterson points out the key of being willing to start over as a novice time and again to find true greatness. If we can learn from others at any stage of life, we are calculated for greatness. The self-imposed fool becomes the master of all.

Note - Nothing's worse than someone who can't possibly see anything they're currently doing wrong. Failure can be a good teacher. It is a stamp of maturity to accept sunk costs, to accept that you were wrong, to accept that you were not perfectly wise, and to move forward in a different direction even when it hurts to do so rather than to stay where you are. People who can't admit they were wrong often live a life of resentment and chronic disappointment. The question we must all ask ourselves is: how much more of our lives are we going to waste?

An Australian school headmaster Robert Grant was known to say, **"I hope your child will be severely disappointed by his time at this school."** This was a way of saying your kid needs to learn that there are hard things in life. That if a kid does not experience disappointment in school, he will be unprepared for it when it comes in real life (where the consequences are bigger.) That he will react with **quitting rather than more trying** when he fails if he has no experience with hardship (and being in over his head). The right kind of education should prepare your kid to handle failure, to slip **loose of a dream when the dream is over** and move to another field of endeavor with no loss of enthusiasm. Many schools now, especially in America, don't teach kids any life skills because they're too busy preparing them to get grades. *(Note – and too busy giving higher grades than kids deserve.)*

A movie called Flashdance features a character telling another, 'if you give up on your dream you die.' These false ideas are pushed, that if you work hard enough it will happen, that if you build it they will come. Parents are also often stuck in this toxic script which only allows one trajectory, one storyline. It's toxic for the same reason that social media is: It's all about me, my success. They equate fulfillment with personal success.

Note - Mother Teresa taught that we should not try to find how far along we are on the journey, we should just keep serving. This is a brilliant focus on what matters most - everything but the self. It's also very empowering as we realize how bad we have screwed up, to turn the page, allow God to forgive, and just go serve. God never intends us to be discouraged.

Teach kids to focus on who they are, not what they do.

Note- this is not to say teach kids to be self-centered narcissists, it is to say that they need to understand their character matters more than their achievements.

Endless achievements won't lead to fulfillment.
It's about who you truly are not who you pretend to be, even if you never get noticed for your integrity. Life is not a movie about your personal success.

Sometimes responsible parents tell kids that their dreams won't come true, that they need to find another dream. Parents afraid of their authority will never **speak these difficult truths**, but if they don't, who will?

There's no point in letting your kids do what they desire if you have not **first educated that desire.** Once desire has been educated, youth can enjoy leisure time more fully.

Parents must instill **meaning** in children; without meaning kids are more likely to become anxious and depressed. Once kids have a sense of meaning they can pursue achievement with confidence because they know why that achievement is worth pursuing. *(Note – it has been said that someone with a sufficient 'why' can*

endure almost any 'what.' This is the fire of the covenant! This is the great mystery of how the saints do what they do. It is the visions of glory!)

The main purpose of school is not to prepare for university but to prepare for life. The purpose of life involves **meaningful work, loving someone, and supporting a cause**. When your kid wants to know **why they should work hard at school you need to be able to answer with a bigger** picture than just getting into college and making a good living. Teach them that experience matters more than acquisition. The most **serious consequence of shifting to a peer-oriented society** is that the **parent** is **no longer able to provide the big picture** about what really matters. Peers simply can't provide this.

K-12 is now a race to nowhere. They're in a **rat race** to get good grades, to go to a good college, but they have no idea **why** beyond the **vague promise** of a comfortable job at the end of the rainbow, and the lack of any coherent alternative.

Pursuing fame wealth and good looks (as pop culture insists) for their own sake impoverishes the soul.

Note – Babylon has it's counterfeit to each noble trait. Beauty thrift industry and influence are all essential elements of Zion, but Babylon's version of them is a sad counterfeit which cannot bring lasting fulfillment and save the souls of men.

Set meaningful goals and work toward them with integrity.

Conclusion

We must recreate a culture of respect as was depicted in old time movies like The Andy Griffith show. Movie characters used to be good role models for kids.

The word **ordinary has become a derogatory** term synonymous with meaninglessness. *(Note – we strive for greatness, but the secret is that greatness isn't how the world sees it, it is manifest in the simple honest Christian life.)*

Your neighbors are **going to accuse you of isolating** your kids. But you can be courageous for your child's sake so they can grow up to be brave and humble like you.

Note – One often ridiculed parenting method is homeschooling. Particularly in today's society of permissiveness and anti-Christianity, homeschooling can be an effective tool to enhance family bonding, enhance individualized learning, enhance family culture being passed on to the next generation, enhance respect, enhance peer group selection via other intentional groups not just random kids from the neighborhood, etc. Homeschooling isn't for everyone but be aware of the ways you need to fortify your family.

Don't try to be authoritative one moment and cool the next. Your job is to be the authoritative parent, not the cool peer.

There are three things emphasized in this book unique to America:

1. The culture of disrespect and 'live for now;' letting kids do whatever they want.
2. The use of powerful psychiatric drugs are a first rather than a last resort.
3. Over-scheduling our kids and ourselves. Rather than boasting about how busy you are, boast about lying on the grass looking for shapes in the clouds with your kids.

There is no greater responsibility between human beings than that of a parent to a child. *(Note – hungry for leadership and influence? Here it is, hiding in plain sight.)* The parents must not only feed and clothe children, but instill in them virtue, a longing for integrity, and the meaning of life.

The collapse of parenting has led to an explosion, particularly in America, of fragile medicated children. You must **create an alternative culture in your home** and exert **without apology** the **primacy of family ties**.

Note- consider modifying holiday traditions, weekly routines, sabbath observance, etc.

Teaching children virtue and character is not an extracurricular optional activity for superior parents, it is the **duty of all parents notwithstanding their imperfection**. This is a mandatory assignment, we cannot abdicate it to others.

Part 3: Supplemental Essays

Kids Won't Spontaneously Learn to Be Good – Joseph Smith Quote

"If children are to be brought up in the way they should go, to be good citizens here and happy hereafter, they must be taught. It is idle to suppose that children will grow up good, while surrounded with wickedness, without cultivation. It is folly to suppose that they can become learned without education."
 --Discourses of the Prophet Joseph Smith, p. 273

Teaching Boys to Become Men by Andrew Skousen
From the World Affairs Brief, 11.25.22

Dominance: Males of many species naturally assert themselves against the male leaders above them, challenging the old dogs, billy goats, rams, bulls, lions, etc. for the top spot. This natural competition has to be schooled into positive directions. Ultimately it should transform into leadership ability—leadership over their family and sometimes other people, activities, or business pursuits. True leadership is not based on charisma, physical prowess or popular appeal, great leaders are marked by how well they indicate the path of truth and inspire righteous action.

Anger: Anger has been universally condemned as a vice, but it is a natural emotion within all of us that, if harnessed with self-control, can be a powerful force for good. Like fire, anger can hurt and harm, but when controlled it is a source of power both to fight against evil, and shape and motivate ourselves and others. The Bible has many references to the "fury" of the Lord reflecting his powerful sense righteous indignation targeting evil actions of people against the innocent.

Anger must be tempered by good judgment and self-control. When used appropriately, you will not be ashamed at how you used it. Even Jesus showed carefully controlled anger toward sometimes lazy apostles, selfish moneychangers in the temple, and especially conspiring sinful Jewish leaders who also plotted his death. In each instance, He only spoke the truth, called them to repentance, and avoided any petty actions. Boys need to learn how to control hotheaded anger by recognizing where they or others made mistakes and work on judgment and allegiance to the truth of the matter to handle it appropriately.

Aggression is a side of anger that especially needs to be controlled. But it is also important in moments of self-defense, when evil people intend to harm us, our family, or innocent bystanders. Even when aggressively defending yourself or others don't let it cloud your judgment; Good firearm and martial arts training teaches to keep a clear head. Occasionally even explosive anger is needed at the right time to destabilize an opponent's control over you or to scare away a wild animal.

Physical desires: Everyone has to learn how to control physical appetites through self-control. Idle hands quickly become "the devil's tools" so expect them to always be engaged in valuable pursuits including chores, schoolwork, practicing musical instruments and learning a foreign language.

As boys mature, they have to master increased hormones and attractions. Chaste behavior is easier without the provocative images prevalent in modern TV, movies, music and social media today. Keep bad influences out of the house and filter and monitor all internet activities. Fill the entertainment void with wholesome books, movies and music. The better you can keep a high standard of living, the easier time they will have controlling these desires. Don't worry, you won't shield them entirely. When the modern world creeps in take the time to teach them about the deeper problems involved and how to avoid it. Eventually, activities and extra-curricular events will bring them in more contact with outside influences, but by then they will be more mature. Teach boys to be courteous and well-mannered, including the lost art of gentleman manners like opening a door for a lady, and treating them respectfully—traits that have been lost in today's world of "equality."

Pride: True pride is the same as true humility: knowing who you are and what you are worth, no more and no less. Too many young men gauge their value by peers' opinions of them, driving them to please friends. Your true ultimate worth is a reflection of God's approval and disapproval depending on our actions, intentions and desires. Accurate pride is seeing ourselves in this honest appraisal of our goodness and abilities. Parents can reinforce this by reflecting the positive and negative reaction of God to a boy's decisions and attitudes, carefully praising when appropriate, and correcting bad decisions.

Boys' proper pride naturally grows when they contribute in meaningful ways, and see the fruit of their labors. If your boys don't want to help out, or do a good job, don't just let them off the hook by doing it for them. They need to gain the self-respect of a job well done. Often this involves learning to push themselves to do hard things. Sometimes it is appropriate to step in to help them after they are already making a full-fledged effort, to help them finish or polish up a task properly, but don't let them get dependent on your help if they are capable of doing it.

Eventually pride will turn into **honor**. True honor is independent of people's accolades, and is inherent in honorable, unimpeachable actions. Honor is sometimes confused with blind patriotism to a country or cause, but this connection is only appropriate when the country or cause is also good. Honor is not rigid pride—it allows for humility, self-correction and asking for forgiveness when in error. Boys need to see proper honor modeled

103

by their father, and be expected to do the honorable action and be taught why.

Hold On To Your Kids - Abbreviated Highlights

Why Parents Need To Matter More Than Peers by Gordon Neufeld and Gabor Mate

When children become more attached to peers than family, it is like having an affair. Ch.2

"It is generally unrecognized by parents and professionals that the root of the problem is not parental ineptitude but parental impotence in the strictest meaning of that word: lacking sufficient power. The absent quality is power, not love or knowledge or commitment or skill. Our predecessors had much more power than parents today. In getting children to heed, our grandparents wielded more power than our parents could exercise over us or we seem to have over our children." (Ch.4)

Peer oriented kids don't care about the Bible or great art and classics, "They know only what is current and popular, appreciate only what they can share with their peers." (Ch. 7)

Note – Since kids want to learn things they can discuss/share with their peers, try to find a good peer group. For example, how comfortable is this peer with discussing the scriptures? It's important to focus on peer groups who are hand selected not just public-school geographic peers, and this is usually done today by finding groups through media and meeting whenever you can.

Note - One tip of course is to go to a geographic location where you're going to find higher quality people, and no that doesn't necessarily mean more money, in fact the opposite might be the case. Though I must say everywhere I look I still haven't found Zion. Brigham Young said we never yet have fully organized a branch of the church, and it sure would be nice if we could, but the people won't have it. I love the community the church makes but I know there is much more to a true religious community when we as a people are ready for it.

Note – When it comes to children wanting to learn things they can share with peers, consider the master weapon of having large family sizes. When children have many peers from their own siblings group the children then have other peers to play with and talk to that have similar values and similar schooling and interests etc.

Attachment with a parent makes the stress of peers ignoring them, taunting, etc. bearable in many ways; it is a shield of protection. (Ch. 8)

Children have always snubbed, ignored, shunned,

shamed other children but in these days children do not have the attachment to family to override the impact of peer acceptance or rejection. (Ch. 8)

"It is not friends that children need... Until children are capable of true friendship, they really do not need friends, just attachments." (Ch. 17)

When Kids Don't Want Religion

Elder Bruce R McConkie said to his kids, 'you have agency, you can come to church and not like it or come to church and like it.'

Church is about so much more than worship of Christ. It is family culture. The family uses church to help each member become their best self, a good citizen, socially armed, versed in letters, of a good temper, and so forth.

As the guardians of that child, you have the legal right to insist on their attendance with you wherever you go.

Even family scripture study can be a requirement. This is a discussion of life, a time of teaching correct principles. It can be done during a family meal to support schedules and unwillingness. At the meal the child doesn't leave until excused.

The child must understand: church is but a small part of the family culture. It looks like it pervades everything (because it does), but it's not just worship of Christ we refer to when we speak of church and religion. Our religion is what tells us how to live. It's the how to live that takes up all our time and directs the way we do everything. If they have an issue with the way we do everything, even if you deleted the church element, the faith in Christ, there's still so much going on. There's how to sleep, how to eat, how to learn, how to play, how to work, how to wear clothes, etc. (like Tevye said).

Our culture is founded in religion, and don't think that just getting rid of religion is going to get rid of all the

culture! Just quitting religion isn't going to save you in this family! We live our religion constantly, and it's not just prayers!

You don't have to believe in God, but you do have to abide by our expectations and culture. When you move out, sure, you can leave all that behind. But we hope that by then, you will have learned a deep sense of gratitude toward us parents for what we have chosen to do for you, and that you will have learned the wisdom in what we have been teaching you, enough to adopt many of these practices into your life.

Helen Keller Training: Strict Works

Once I showed some students a film about the training of Helen Keller. One student commented, "This is when teachers were allowed to discipline their students." Precisely. And that is why Sullivan had tremendous success with Keller, and why we are having little success with you! (I didn't say that to the lad, but it was sort of understood anyway.) Everyone saw the success this teacher was having and knew their teachers don't have much success, and nodded their heads.

In one depiction of the Hellen Keller story, Hellen's father sees Sullivan struggling with the child, and says, "do you even like her?" Sullivan responds, "do you?" The truth is, that when a child is completely out of control, no one likes them! Only when order is established can peace prevail. Training and enforced boundaries are needed.

Sullivan pointed out that she needed complete control over her pupil (Hellen) if she was to be able to teach her pupil. She knew that there couldn't just be a soft way out. There needed to be real, and even harsh consequences for noncompliance. Sullivan knew that hardship makes someone strong, and the role of a teacher is to make a pupil strong, so the teacher must put the student through something hard. In today's world, teachers and parents don't have complete control over their pupils, and the training abilities are limited.

Obviously, it's good to have some basic standards to protect children; but what's happening goes far beyond that and makes the state more of the parent than the actual parent. In other words, decisions about your child are being made by a team of unconcerned unrelated socialists who don't have a clue about real child development or faith.

CS Lewis on Not Being a Pacifist - Highlights Abbreviated

Just because war doesn't solve all of our problems doesn't mean that it doesn't solve some of them; for example, if you defend yourself from a tiger that's still a good thing even though it didn't cure your rheumatism.

History is full of useless wars as well as useful wars.

Sometimes to help one person you must do violence to another person.

In some instances death penalty may be the only sufficient method of respect. The death sentence is not just an expression of fear it is an expression of the importance of high morals that need to be defended.

Oppression is a greater evil than death and pain. The question is not whether war is a great evil, the question is, is war the greatest evil.

Note: When there are unideal situations we have to use unideal methods as those are the only methods which you have at your disposal to meet the demands of that situation. In other words, what isn't an ideal method in one scenario can be an ideal method in another. The greater evil would be allowing chaos and danger to prevail. Allowing anarchy and brewing contempt.

Only liberal societies tolerate pacifists. Pacifist states are handed over to their totalitarian neighbors. A pacifist state is a straight road to a world where there will be no pacifists.

.Note – Ghandi's methods worked against the mostly benevolent British, they would not have worked against many of the more ruthless countries untampered by Judeo-Christian values.

If you think that there's never righteous war you have to part with all the great literature, and all the great philosophers. He quotes one who said, "If you will not take the universal opinion of mankind I have no more to say."

Jesus said pacifist things, but those must be taken with qualification. If you just take single things that Jesus said and apply them alone, you also have plenty of other difficult things including not pacifist things to abide by. Yes we turn the other cheek, but there are obvious exceptions. Obviously Jesus did **not mean that when**

110

raising a child to just let that child hit its parents whenever it wants, or to just give your child whatever it wants.

Jesus' teaching is clear, we should control our anger. How we respond to something depends on the situation because there legitimately may be another reason for retaliating than egotistic anger. When you hit back but not in egotistic anger you can in fact be justified.

Many people have tried to have their own unbalanced flavor of Jesus: the liberal Jesus, the Marxist Jesus, all kinds of different Jesus' that people promote.

Note: The Book of Mormon gives us the true Jesus, and affirms the once clear and accepted testimony of the bible. The point of the Book of Mormon is to get people to believe the bible again, and to cast down the uninspired interpretations of the bible which prevail today.

Don't Be Soft on Crime

Kent Hovind points out that it is a communist idea to be soft on crime, things like '3 strikes you're out.' This tramples on **victims' rights**.

Cleon Skousen as chief of police of SLC Utah had to deal with crime with a firm hand, and the crime and homelessness and prostitution was virtually eliminated. People complained that he was too strict, and he was released from office, after which the crime quickly returned.

A retired police officer from Washington told me we are the first nation in the history of the world that has made **punishment painless**. He says we aren't deterring crime, and the criminals are overrunning us. He says police in big cities aren't allowed to do their job. He says that many a man has been made experiencing consequences, and we are now robbing of them of that opportunity.

Ogletree's 7 Mistakes LDS Parents Make

Ideas from Mark Ogletree PhD for Latter-day Saint parents. Compare them and think of your own list to sure up your parenting methods.

1. Not teaching your children how to work effectively.

2. Teaching children that obedience is optional. (allowing disobedience contributes to disobedience)

3. Protecting children from anything they don't want to do, or anything that is hard, uncomfortable, or inconvenient. (Homework, participation, etc.)

4. Teaching your children that agency means freedom.

5. Teaching your children that you will be there to solve every problem.

6. Sheltering children from rejection and disappointment. ("Trophies all around")

7. Teaching your children that they don't need a testimony right now—it can wait until they are older.

(Ogletree's full article is at http://www.ldsliving.com/7-Mistakes-LDS-Parents-Make-and-How-to-Avoid-Them/s/78481/?utm_source=ldsliving&utm_medium=sidebar&utm_campaign=related)

Randal's 25 Mistakes LDS Parents Make

From book "The 25 Mistakes LDS Parents Make and How to Avoid Them book by Randal A. Wright, PhD. Randal is a long-time social scientist and church member who has worked teaching in the CES program.

Compare them and think of your own list to sure up your parenting methods.

1. Home environment (that reflects the gospel)
2. Quality time (and quantity)
3. The crossroads (be there at critical times)
4. Family traditions (have them to teach, indoctrinate, & unify)
5. Children's friends (don't allow them to associate too closely with those who don't share their values)
6. Peer pressure (teach how to deal with it)
7. Television (limit exposure, none in bedrooms)
8. Music (limit access to inappropriate)
9. Movies (prevent exposure to inappropriate)
10. Parental example
11. Expressing love verbally (daily to family members)
12. Physical affection (give it)
13. Support (each other's events, games, & activities)
14. Marriage (build it strong to show how it works)
15. Family fun (& laughter)
16. Discipline (be consistent, non-harsh, non-lax)
17. Worldly heroes (discourage over-involvement)
18. Teaching correct principles (don't assume church & society will)

19. Human intimacy (teach the importance and proper role)

20. Steady dating (prohibit during teen years)

21. Underage dating (before 16)

22. Communication (keep the lines open with your children)

23. Self-worth (build a positive self-image in your children)

24. Spiritual experiences (take advantage of inspired church-sponsored programs)

25. Warning signs (recognize)

Loving Parenting: Quotes from Early Latter-day Saint Leaders

A balance of love and limits is needed in parenting. First lets look at these quotes on loving parenting:

"Nothing is so much calculated to lead people to forsake sin as to take them by the hand, and watch over them with tenderness. When persons manifest the least kindness and love to me, O what power it has over my mind, while the opposite course has a tendency to harrow up all the harsh feelings and depress the human mind" (*Teachings of the Prophet Joseph Smith,* sel. Joseph Fielding Smith [1976], 240) (Cited in Eternal Marriage manual, "Parenthood: Creating a Gospel Centered Home"; see https://www.lds.org/manual/eternal-marriage-student-manual/parenthood-creating-a-gospel-centered-home?lang=eng)

"It is not by the whip or the rod that we can make obedient children; but it is by faith and by prayer, and by setting a good example before them" (Brigham Young, Deseret News Weekly, 9 Aug. 1865, 3)

"Parents should never drive their children, but lead them along, giving them knowledge as their minds are prepared to receive it. Chastening may be necessary betimes, but parents should govern their children by faith rather than by the rod, leading them kindly by good example into all truth and holiness" (*Discourses of Brigham Young,* sel. John A. Widtsoe [Salt Lake City: Deseret Book Co., 1941], p. 208). (This is cited in the Parent Guide LDS manual)

"That President Young lived the principles he taught is evidenced by his daughter Susa's description of him as "an ideal father. Kind to a fault, tender, thoughtful, just and firm. … None of us feared him; all of us adored him" (*LSBY,* 356)" (Teachings of the Presidents of the Church: Brigham Young, Ch 46 "Parental Responsibility"; see https://www.lds.org/manual/teachings-brigham-young/chapter-46?lang=eng)

"I will here say to parents, that kind words and loving actions towards children, will subdue their uneducated natures a great deal better than the rod, or, in other words, than physical punishment. Although it is written that, "The rod and reproof give wisdom; but a child left to himself bringeth his mother to shame," and, "he that spareth his rod hateth his son; but he that loveth him chasteneth him betimes;" these quotations refer to wise and prudent corrections. **Children who have lived in the sunbeams of parental kindness and affection, when made aware of a parent's displeasure, and receive a kind reproof from parental lips, are more thoroughly chastened, than by any physical punishment** that could be applied to their persons. It is written, that the Lord "shall smite the earth with the rod of his mouth." And again it is written, "a whip for the horse, a bridle for the ass, and a rod for the fool's back." The rod of a parent's mouth, when used in correction of a beloved child, is more potent in its effects, than the rod which is used on the fool's back. When children are reared under the rod, which is for the fool's back, it not unfrequently occurs, that they become so stupified and lost to every high-toned feeling and sentiment, that though you bray them in a mortar among wheat with a pestle, yet will not their foolishness depart from them. Kind looks, kind actions, kind words, and a lovely, holy deportment towards them, will bind our children to us with bands that cannot easily be broken; while abuse and unkindness will drive them from us, and break asunder every holy tie, that should bind them to us, and to the everlasting covenant in which we are all embraced. **If my family; and my brethren and sisters, will not be obedient to me on the basis of kindness, and a commendable life before all men, and before the heavens, then farewell to all influence.** Earthly kings and potentates obtain influence and power by terrorism, and maintain it by the same means. Had I to obtain

117

power and influence in that way, I should never possess it in this world nor in the next. Fathers who send their little boys and girls on the plains and ranges, to herd their cattle and sheep, and drag them out of bed very early in the morning, to go out in the cold and wet, perhaps without shoes and but scantily clad otherwise, are cruel to their offspring, and when their children arrive at years of maturity, they will leave the roof under which they have received such oppression, and free themselves from the control of parents, who have acted towards them, **more like task-masters than natural protectors.** It is in this unnatural school that our **thieves have their origin**, and where they receive their first lessons in dishonesty and wild recklessness. Mark the path in which a number of our boys have travelled, from the time they were eight or ten years of age, to sixteen, eighteen and twenty. **Have they been caressed and kindly treated** by their parents, sent to school, and when at home taught to read good books, taught to pray themselves, and to hear their parents pray? **Have they been accustomed to live and breathe in a peaceful, quiet, heavenly influence when at home? No. Then can you wonder that your children are wild, reckless and ungovernable?** They care not for a name, or standing in society, every noble aspiration is blunted; for they are made to go here or there, like mere machines, at the beck and call of tyrant parents, and are uncultivated and uncivilized. This picture will apply to a few of our young men. Let parents treat their children as they themselves would wish to be treated, and set an example before them that is worthy of you as Saints of God. Parents are responsible before the Lord, for the way in which they educate and train their children, for "Lo, children are an heritage of the Lord; and the fruit of the womb is his reward. Happy is the man that hath his quiver full of them; they shall not be ashamed, but they shall speak with the enemies in the gate." (Brigham Young, Journal of Discourses Vol. 10, 360-362; find it here https://www.fairmormon.org/answers/Journal_of_Discourses/10/66) (a portion of the above quote is also featured in Teachings of the Presidents of the Church: Brigham Young, Ch 46 https://www.lds.org/manual/teachings-brigham-young/chapter-46?lang=eng)

Strict Parenting Quotes from Early Latter-day Saint Leaders

Now that we have looked at a few quotes on loving parenting, lets balance the equation by showcasing a few quotes on setting limits in parenting:

"You ought always to take the lead of your children in their minds and affections. **Instead of being behind with the whip**, always be in advance, then you can say, "Come along," and you will have no use for the rod. They will delight to follow you, and will like your words and ways, because you are always comforting them and giving them pleasure and enjoyment. **If they get a little naughty, stop them when they have gone far enough.** … When they transgress, and transcend certain bounds we want them to stop. If you are in the lead they will stop, they cannot run over you; but if you are behind they will run away from you." (*DNSW*, 8 Dec. 1868, 2–3) (also cited in Teachings of the Presidents of the Church: Brigham Young, Ch 46 https://www.lds.org/manual/teachings-brigham-young/chapter-46?lang=eng)

"I tell the mothers **not to allow the children to indulge in evils**, but at the **same time to treat them with mildness**. If a child is required to step in a certain direction, and it does not seem willing to do so, **gently put it in the desired way**, and say, There, my little dear, you must step when I speak to you. Children need directing and teaching what is right in a kind, affectionate manner." (*DBY,* 209) (also cited in Teachings of the Presidents of the Church: Brigham Young, Ch 46 https://www.lds.org/manual/teachings-brigham-young/chapter-46?lang=eng)

"Truly He loves us, and because He loves us, He neither compels nor abandons us. Rather He helps and guides us. Indeed, **the real manifestation of God's love is His commandments**." (Elder Christofferson "Free Forever to Act for Themselves," Oct. 2014 Conf. Report)

"No man can ever become a ruler in the Kingdom of God, until he can perfectly rule himself; then is he capable of raising a family of children who will rise up and call him blessed" (*Discourses of Brigham Young,* 265; cited in Eternal Marriage manual, see https://www.lds.org/manual/eternal-marriage-student-manual/parenthood-creating-a-gospel-centered-home?lang=eng).

"As parents, we are sometimes **too intimidated to teach or testify to our children.** I have been guilty of that in my own life. Our children need to have us share spiritual feelings with them and to teach and bear testimony to them." (Robert D Hales in Conference Report, Apr. 1999, 41–44; or *Ensign,* May 1999, 33–34; Cited in Eternal Marriage manual, "Parenthood: Creating a Gospel Centered Home"; see https://www.lds.org/manual/eternal-marriage-student-manual/parenthood-creating-a-gospel-centered-home?lang=eng)

Joel Skousen on Conscience Training

The following are highlights from Joel's landmark essay on conscience, available at JoelSkousen.com in text and audio.

Don't let something nag on, make peace, set the boundary, then all can feel safe and be calm. Peace is when there is order. There is no peace without order. Constant negotiating isn't peace.

People who think well know that it is an active process. Control and analyze what you think about force yourself to be aware of and analyze every thought to determine its credibility.

Replace things which aren't inherently wrong, but which are not as productive as other things you could be doing. Conscience is about helping you sort out conflicting priorities.

God tests us by seeing whether we will act on the good promptings or the bad promptings they both sound like your own voice.

Parents often become so **desensitized** to conscience that the **bad behavior of their children doesn't bother them enough** to stop it. Parents often feel the guilt of being too strict but they're often **not sensitive enough to feel the guilt of being too permissive**.

Have a list of constructive things your children can learn and do in their spare time. Then train them to discipline themselves about what they should be doing, to feel what they've left undone, etc.

You don't have to be a rule making and legalistic society when you train to listen to conscience; do this training by giving little promptings to your children frequently, asking how they're feeling about certain things, and telling them how you the as the parent are feeling about what they should do.

Much **societal withdrawal is needed for children** as they haven't yet learned to resist evil. This is why homeschooling is popular among conscious parents.

When you accept a chronic issue as something you can't overcome, you have dulled your conscience.

Quotes on Ensuring Recreation is Wholesome

"It is impossible to unite Christ and Baal – their spirits cannot unite, their objects and purposes are entirely different; the one leads to eternal life and exaltation, the other to death and final destruction." (Brigham Young, JD vol. 11; "Union. Persecution. The Nature of the Kingdom of God.)

"Refrain from illusions and seek divine and scientific truth" – Mother of Dimitri Mendeleev, her last words to him.

"Too often we use many hours for fun and pleasure, clothed in the euphemism 'I'm recharging my batteries.' Those hours could be spent reading and studying to gain knowledge, skills, and culture." (President Henry B Eyring in "Today's Family: Chose Wholesome Recreation" https://www.churchofjesuschrist.org/prophets-and-apostles/unto-all-the-world/choose-wholesome-recreation?lang=eng

"That which does not edify is not of God and is darkness." (D&C 50:23).

"I give not unto you that ye shall live after the manner of the world." D&C 93:13.

"We should train ourselves to find pleasure in that which invigorates, not stupefies and destroys the body; that which leads upward and not down; that which brightens, not dulls and stunts the intellect; that which elevates and exalts the spirit, not that clogs and depresses it. So shall we please the Lord, enhance our own enjoyment, and save ourselves and our children from impending sins..." (Joseph F Smith Answers to Gospel Questions, vol. 1 (SLC Deseret Book 1957) p92.)

"One's character may be determined in some measure by the quality of one's amusements." And "Tell me what amusements you like best and whether your amusements have become a ruling passion in your life, and I will tell you what you are." (Joseph F Smith, "The Social Effects of Card Playing" in Juvenile Instructor, Vol. 38, Sept. 1, 1903, 528-529)

[Avoid] whatever weakens your reason, whatever impairs the tenderness of your conscience, whatever obscures your sense of God, whatever takes off your relish for spiritual things, whatever increases the authority of the body over the mind. (See Ezra Taft Benson, "In His Steps," Speeches of the Year, 1979 [Provo: Brigham Young University Press, 1980], p. 61.)

Additional Insights on Ensuring Recreation is Wholesome

Video games are dangerous on many levels, but particularly in that most kids get **addicted** to them; most of them are **frivolous**. Simulations of real-life things could work on some level, but still, we see desensitization to life when we are so frequently **engulfed** in the fantastic and abnormal. Some argue that gaming gives people skills, but throwing a ball and many other more natural things (which don't have the side effects the games do) also will improve your skills in similar ways. You don't want kids living in the virtual world, that's not how to get the most out of life.

Popular music these days has these **2 themes**: **1. Do it your way, 2. Don't worry** about the future. AKA, you, not God, are in charge, and God can't get in your way.

In a recent assembly I attended a rocker guy showed up and straight up said 'religion is crap.' Then he gave some watered-down protestant sermon. So, this is what we are authorizing, this false priesthood to preach to our kids at schools. Of course, then come the drag queens, and others eager to teach the philosophies of men mingled with scripture.

School (and often community) **dances** and assemblies are trash, and people pay others to spew this trash (usually your taxes). At the dances these days, young or old, people jump around like primates. Many feel **shy**, which is their **conscience** telling them not to engage in this nonsense. Of course, there is an entire corpus of music about ignoring conscience and loosening up, letting go, etc. Babylon is all about training you how to violate conscience.

Entire genres should be avoided. Some justify listening to poor music around kids by claiming that 'the kids don't **understand** what the song is saying,' but the kids do understand the sound; children's spirits are intelligent, and they'll gravitate to the toxic **culture** the music is always about.

Pokémon characters are all sassy and mean. The whole theme is dark and occultic. The production is **made by same people** who made "Magic the Gathering." Satan is gathering his anti-Christ New Age adherents. Beware of falling into the trap of excessive fantasy and magic rather than focusing on truth.

Pornographic messages and costumes are blended into most anime programs. For example, I was once in a home where an anime program was entertaining small children. Out of nowhere a **random line** of the program joked about taking a picture of a child without her clothes on. It's double speech… I wondered, did anyone else hear that?! The Devil is cunning indeed! Parents are wise to discern which genres have corrupt tendencies and to ban them entirely.

Once when I expressed discomfort about an anime shirt a student of mine was wearing, the student said, "there's **no such thing as Christian anime**." Well put. Anime is based on eastern culture and ideas, and boundaries of gender modesty and respect aren't strong there like in the west. We don't realize how much Judeo-Christian values have impacted our society for the better until we encounter the vanity of cultures which are void of those teachings.

The **danger of all temptation is about trading your power of agency** for some cheap fleeting thrill. So many songs sing "lose control," that's a Satanic message. Brigham talked about this when he said we **shouldn't fly off the handle** in rage (or other emotions), we shouldn't just express every emotion we feel. Rather, we should control ourselves.

Relationship Before Correction: God's Pattern

Joseph Smith reported being rebuked by the Lord on a few occasions, it is a very painful experience. But the reason the Lord could do that with Joseph was the relationship they had.

In the Book of Mormon, the missionaries taught God's plan (his love, the good news of the gospel, their glorious identity and destiny, etc.) BEFORE teaching the commandments.

People these days rarely have relationships. One cannot discipline another without a relationship. Once you have a strong bond, you can teach with strength. If you discern someone is ready, you can give it to them plainly. But for most, we aren't there.

Family must be careful not to destroys family members' sense of self-worth as families are typically too harsh. We say God is love but we don't believe it! Yes, there are rough daily situations where some commands need to be given, but please, let's also turn up the love. Let's make sure amid stressful work projects etc. that everyone is aware of the unchanging love of God for them. Only in the context of God's love can we rise and accomplish the high expectations of the Christian life.

1 2 3 Magic: Effective Discipline for Children 2-12 by Thomas W. Phelan PhD – Book Highlights

Highlights by Beth Richardson, arranged by Nate Richardson

Sections:
Strike out
Administering the time out
Manipulation
Encourage the good

STRIKE OUT

Give 3 strikes, then time out.

Note – another way of seeing 3 strikes is to give a reminder, then a warning, then a consequence.

On the third strike they "take 5" or one minute for each year.

Don't count something as a strike unless you see or hear it.

Start the strikes over after about a half hour of good behavior.

Count strikes when in tricky situations, even in company. If there is a fight between siblings, give strikes to both of them. Don't ask " what happened" or "who started it." Kids excessively goofing off at the meal table can get strikes.

If the child is having a tantrum don't start their timeout time until they are done.

Major rudeness etc. constitutes an automatic strike out.

ADMINISTERING THE TIME OUT

Time out works best in the room where the child is not there in your face trying to argue and make you mad. Other kids who share the room will need to not be in the room. Get valuables out of the room since they may break them when upset. If they pee on the floor, timeouts are in the bathroom. You can use store restrooms if they need timeouts at the store. You can pull over in a car for a timeout.

Don't bring up what happened unless necessary as it makes the child upset again.

Make the time out short. Most kids come out of time out forgetting why they were put there.

If the child does not go to time out when told start moving towards them and they will most likely start moving. If the child is small and they don't go pick them up. If the child is big and they don't go, they give them a TOA's (Time Out Alternative) such as no TV, no friends, toy taken, no desert, early bedtime, extra chores, etc. Let the child pick the TOA. it will help them to be less mad at you.

MANIPULATION

Kids have six main kinds of testing and manipulation:
1. Badgering (saying the same thing over and over).
2. Temper/Intimidation (getting mad).
3. Threatening ("I'm going to run away from home").
4. Martyrdom ("nobody likes me" or " I never get anything").
5. Buttering up ("Mom you have really pretty eyes or " I think I'll go clean my room now"). *(Note- you do the crime, you do the time, even if you suddenly decide to be good afterward.)*
6. Physical tactics (throwing things or hurting the adult)

If a child has a favorite tactic that's bad, because that means it works.

Two big mistakes that parents make when they are mad are too much talking and too much emotion. Remain calm as you give strikes.

Keep it simple like "that's one" when they attempt manipulation, and "that's two" when they continue the manipulation, etc. *Note - They already know they're in the wrong, so your job is to show that you'll follow through, not to keep reteaching what's right and what's wrong.*

If a child comes up to you and asks you for something and you say no and they ask why, give them one explanation then start giving strikes.

When you are dealing with lying remember that it is not the end of the world and that there are worse things. Try not to "corner" or "test" or "impulsively" the child as the child will continue to lie and you are giving your child practices sessions.

Bigger problems like stealing, lying, property damage, bullying, fights, etc. need bigger punishments than time-outs, such as being grounded from electronics for two weeks, extra chores, community service, educational activity (research subject they are struggling with etc.).

ENCOURAGE THE GOOD

Give simple requests, and don't phrase them like questions.

Small children need lots of help and praise (give our praise like candy). Middle age children like charts and timers. Older children do well with natural consequences (encourage them to make better choices next time as they experience natural consequences).

Ask teachers to help you in "independence training" by requiring your child to explain in front of the class (and experience embarrassment) when they are late or do poorly on an assignment.

When kids fail to clean, you can (without complaining) confiscate the messy things until a certain time.

Have a set time for homework (no TV, maybe calm music). Have a set time for bedtime. Announce when these times are. Have a clear bedtime routine list.

Have monthly family meetings to address problems. Also have monthly kid-parent dates.

Give corrections as PNP: Positive Negative Positive. *Note – this is similar to the D&C 121 priesthood revelation, directing people to show love after needed corrections.*

Listen carefully to your children and they'll be more likely to listen to you.

Who's In Charge Around Here?

Why are kids rejecting parental authority and being raised by peers? Dr. Sax has toured around the world and discovered that America is the worst when it comes to permissive parenting, resulting in kids with bad attitudes. He has seen hundreds of cases of parents who treat kids like the kid is the boss, turning decision making over to kids in matters of food, school, friends, and about everything else.

Dr. Sax brings a refreshing voice of reason to empower parents in their mission to lead kids to meaningful success. It's time to take back our role as parents and no longer allow medications, social media, video games, and peers to raise our kids.

Nate contributes unique perspectives from the restored Church of Jesus Christ which work together with highlights from Dr. Sax's work to help parents restore their authority to raise responsible happy kids.

Made in the USA
Columbia, SC
17 December 2024

49474594R00074